Nothing But Brush Strokes

Nothing But Brush Strokes

Selected Prose

Phyllis Webb

The Writer as Critic: V

General Editor
Smaro Kamboureli

NeWest

Canadian Cataloguing in Publication Data

Webb, Phyllis, 1927-
Nothing but brush strokes

(Writer as critic : 5)
Includes bibliographical references and index.
ISBN 0-920897-89-4

I. Title. II. Series: The writer as critic series ; 5
PS8545.E22N67 1995   C818'.54   C95-910728-2
PR9199.3. W43N67 1995

Editor for the press: Smaro Kamboureli
Editorial Coordinator: Eva Radford
Cover: Brenda Burgess / Burgess and Michalchuk
Cover photograph: Destrubé
Book design: John Luckhurst/GDL

Blaser, Robin, "Image-Nation I (the fold," (1962 - 64) from *The Holy Forest*, © 1993 by Robin Blaser. Published by Coach House Press, reprinted by permission.

Printed and bound in Canada

NeWest Publishers Limited
Suite 310, 10359 - 82 Avenue
Edmonton, Alberta T6E 1Z9

For Tiff and Bill
faithful friends

Contents

Preface

If there seems to be a multiple personality running loose in this book, it can probably be explained by the time-span these prose pieces cover—twenty-five years—and the diversity of occasions that called them forth. When I wrote my study of "Cyclic Notions in Proust" in 1970, I was trying to make a living as a free-lance writer and broadcaster, and its first incarnation was as a radio broadcast. I revised it in 1982 for my book *Talking*, now out of print. Other pieces were commissioned: "Phyllis Webb's Canada," "Gabrielle Roy's *Windflower*," "And Things Get Stranger Every Day." Invitations to conferences produced "The Muse Figure" and "The Crannies of Matter"; a trip to Australia for The Adelaide Festival inspired "The Drover's Wife—Again." Being asked to contribute to anthologies resulted in "Message Machine" and "Tibetan Desire," and a fiftieth issue of *Brick* celebration made me tread the tedious shores of "Might-Have-Been." Even *Nothing But Brush Strokes*, this very book, got put together because of an invitation.

"Oh, how lovely to be *wanted*," sighs one of the personalities. "But we won't make it easy for you, stupid," the others snarl. These contenders for my soul are, I hope, just trying to protect the poet person. Or they're a sign, at last recognized, to take a late-life turn towards the visual arts. A few examples of this *tentative* appear later in the collection.

The subjects of these essays are various, but themes and concerns recur, and the focus is usually literary, with a few light brush strokes of fantasy here and there. If the tone- and mood-shifts are frequent, time, place, and my own state of mind might account for some of their occurrences; others were deliberately contrived to keep an audience entertained, or, at the very least, awake. Perhaps I'm best able to relax into my subject when I know there will be a reader who has the leisure and inclination to enter into an imaginary dialogue with the author. Time, then, for me to issue my invitation: may I have the pleasure of your company?

Phyllis Webb
Salt Spring Island, 1995

The Drover's Wife – Again

Hazel and the rotten landscape dominate everything. Gordon, her husband, stares at a reproduction of Drysdale's famous painting called *The Drover's Wife*. I'm not a drover, I'm a *dentist*, Gordon says, grinding his teeth as he thinks of big-boned Hazel and her stained underarm patches. He hates that—her clumsiness, her silliness, her sweat, her gentle face that other women like. Rotten landscape. Rotten Hazel, who walked out on Gordon and their two kids, leaving a note pencilled on butcher paper, *I am just going round the corner.*

Adelaide is a small town. It's been hard for Gordon. She could be anywhere in the vast Australian landscape. She's carrying her suitcase in her left hand, *hiding her ring*, Gordon thinks. He would. Hazel hasn't given a thought to the damned ring since she vamoosed with the drover thirty years ago. That's him in the background now, bending over to feed the horse or adjust its halter. Gordon peers closer: either that man is a small character or it is a ruddy big horse. Gordon pulls out a magnifying glass to get a better look at his rival. Nothing but brush strokes. Well, aren't we all.

But he's drawn again to the figure in the foreground and can see she's still unhappy, has put on weight, just look at her legs. She's leaving again. Or, perhaps, she's uncertain. Distance = doubts.

I have never seen the original of this painting. I am distant and doubting, stealing words from a short story of which no part may be reproduced by any process without written permission from the publisher. I look in vain through Murray Bail's collection of stories for permission given to reproduce in black and white the painting *The Drover's Wife* (20" x 24", 1945) by Russell Drysdale.

I pick up my bag. It's hot. I flick the flies away, which the artist neglected to render. I walk in my sandshoes off the edge of the rotten landscape, nothing but brush strokes, heading for a coral reef, gentle faces. I am just going round the corner—flick, flick—I am just going round the corner. . . .

1992

I make out a boat   the soul's image   a voice a residence
and the disappearance from a work   over the last
blind note   "Oh, a boat of friends"   the music of,
logos of   a blinding instrument   our words, mine
among them   wash at the perilous   social, political,
hellish and heavenly parts

Robin Blaser, "Image-Nation 12 (Actus"

The Muse Figure

Too late I had the best idea: the cast of characters for this little scene should be expanded.

Imagine behind me a raised stage: on it, draped appropriately in soft, flowing Grecian gowns, the nine Muses (each with an alluring bare shoulder revealed), living representatives and their mother Mnemosyne—Memory.

The daughters' names are lovely: Calliope (Epic Poetry), Clio (History), Euterpe (Lyric Poetry), Melpomene (Tragedy), Terpsichore (Choral Dancing), Erato (Erotic Poetry and Mime), Polyhymnia (Sacred Poetry), Urania (Astronomy), and Thaleia (Comedy). One by one they might be coaxed forth to proffer the right word at the right moment, the bright idea in the nick of time, the smile, demure and knowing, the power in the palm of the hand.

But too late for this frustrated stage director to enhance our occasion. You are left with only me—mortal, human, and to you the entirely fallible.

For me, the Muse figure has never figured as a potent imaginative presence, but the best advice I ever heard her give was to that marvelous and silky poet of the sixteenth century, Sir Philip Sidney, when in a fit of bad temper, she said to him (I think with some disdain), "Fool! . . . look in thy heart, and write."

Let me make it clear that I'm not sure just how much Sir Philip Sidney's muse was the function of a literary convention. I and you will never know if his and other male poets' references to the Muse or Muses was like a close encounter of a third kind, or simply a literary ritual gesture to prove they knew the rules of the game they were playing.

What I think I do know about writers of our own time leads me to believe that we (and I mean men and women) do not have muses. We have psychology and "shrinks," lovers and pets, but we do not have muses. We have drugs and alcohol and money; we have gurus, astral travel, and Carl Sagan. We have *Columbus* and *Challenger*. Have or had Marilyn and Bogey, the Dukes of Hazzard and the Dupes of Dallas, but we do not have muses.

The Muse was once regarded as the source of truth. Truth, according to Robert Graves, "was represented by poets as a naked woman—a woman divested of all garments or ornaments that might commit her," Graves says, rather daringly, I think, "to any particular position in time and space." She is, says the author of *The White Goddess*, anti-domestic, the perpetual "other woman." Right away you can see the problem she poses to the contemporary woman poet/writer, who herself may be anti-domestic, even the other woman, if not exactly the awful and naked Truth.

"The myths are wearing thin," Graves writes, and indeed they are. Or some are. The myth and reality of the "other woman" still prevail in our imaginative lives, though the other woman today might mean not mistress-lover but radical feminist. How telling that phrase is, "the other woman": she is other, a/part. But according to the ancient tradition of myth and psyche, she is also various and in her cruelest aspect (enter hag, witch, bitch, and whore) she is also the "dark executioner" and "supplanter," the Night-Mare who fills her nest with the jawbones and entrails of poets. Oh vain and heartless darling! The angel/devil who refuses to live in the house. "Impartial, loving, severe, wise," she's also devouring, yummy, castrating, and just plain mean, a projection of the male psyche to be coaxed, wooed, feared and honoured, invoked and set aside when the work is done. She is carnal knowledge and inspired divinity. "Fool, . . . look in thy heart, and write." One can understand the tone of disdain, the boredom of it all.

Well, I have looked in my heart and written, and yet why do I so often feel that something or someone else is writing the poem? Why do I sometimes hear a voice calling "Phyllis," calling me to my senses, to my self? One could turn to Jung for that answer, or to Julian Jaynes and his theory about the right side of the brain. One could look at the whole shamanic tradition—and all these things I hope we'll do.

But let me turn briefly for a closer look at that portentous figure Mnemosyne, the mother of the Muses. Did she come from Herland that she produced only daughters? She represented Memory at a time in the mind and life of humankind or unkind when not being able to read was not termed illiteracy; when calendars were not handed out at the local bank; when there were no tape-recorders, phonograph records, not even books. She was It. *Speak, Memory*, Vladimir Nabokov's autobiography, was originally called, *Speak, Mnemosyne*, but Nabokov was told that "little old ladies would not want to ask for a book whose title they could not pronounce." Presumably little old men would be able to pronounce it. Memory *is* life—we need it not only for the recall and perpetuation of our own lives, but for the celebrations, lamentations and history of the tribe, the nation and the world. But the *grande dame* Mnemosyne is almost dead.

The original Muses might be imaged now as little Apples, home-computers wired into the great mother memory bank of the world, promiscuously fingered by the swift digits of the global villagers. But a computer does not a muse or music make.

What then of the bemused heart Sir Philip Sidney's Muse commanded him to look into? His own reflection? Even at the risk of narcissism—and I've always been grateful that Narcissus was a man—we must look there in the pool of the heart, for I think this so-called "heart" has something to do with the individual consciousness and the individual talent. I think it feeds on memory, hears the bicameral voices of the old brain, and it speaks back, speaks a very special kind of memory, ancient and modern, male and female. It will even give a tiny futuristic squeak, or is it a scream, if you breathe very deeply and say, "Remember, Tomorrow."

1983

Waterlily and Multifoliate Rose: Cyclic Notions in Proust

Midway this way of life we're bound upon
I woke to find myself in a dark wood,
Where the right road was wholly lost and gone.

I did not have to reach Dante's "Midway this way to life" to experience the dark wood, the lost way. If lostness returns, recurs, and becomes the problematical, then one learns ways out, though I don't, and few do find their way to Dante's Rose of Paradise. And, as Proust says, "the only true paradise is always the paradise we have lost." You can't go home again, but the way out is sometimes via the way back. And so, that summer I moved to Salt Spring Island, my kind of paradise and easy to reach. But this isn't about my dark wood and lost road—only in the path of those things, and how, in a period of desolation between poems, those cyclic, seemingly barren periods when all is meaningless, I finally read Proust.

Over the past twenty years or so I have tried at least three or four times to read Marcel Proust's *Remembrance of Things Past*. I managed *Swann's Way* and *Within a Budding Grove*, the first two books. I was not ripe enough, or found Proust's temperament alien to mine, or didn't have the patience to stay with him to pursue his grand design, and I never read the entire book. Now, for some reason, I took the books up again, wound myself finally around this intricately designed cycle of novels. It was the month of August. My equivalent to Proust's cork-lined room in Paris a seventeen-foot trailer overlooking Fulford Harbour. A world so different from the intensely social one of Proust's novel, I experienced a delicious disharmony as I looked up from his pages to the beach below where the herons stood on their tall legs fishing, where surf-scoters bobbed, clams spurted; where I could put down the book and walk and stare at stones, stumble through weeds of mud flats, watch ferries pass. And remember my past. Or try not to remember my past. But knowing as I walked and watched that I was looking for something, an unmethodical research was going on. Back with the book, it became evident that in *Remembrance of Things Past* a similar but methodical research on a grand scale was in progress.

A la Recherche du Temps Perdu, Proust's title, loses something in translation. *Remembrance of Things Past* is a poetic equivalent from Shakespeare's Sonnet XXX, "When to the sessions of sweet silent thought / I summon up remembrance of things past. . . ." But the rich reverberations that "*recherche*" sends out—search, quest, pursuit, and the more rigorous research, investigation, examination—are missing in the English title. And though in the French the "past" may be implied in "*perdu*," "*perdu*" actually means lost, wasted, ruined, undone, dead, destroyed, doomed, invisible, forlorn, stray. And "Things" of the English title has to substitute for "time" in the French, the book's central theme, time and timeless art:

> The grandeur of real art . . . is to rediscover, grasp again, and lay before us that reality from which we live so far removed and from which we become more and more separated as the formal knowledge which we substitute for it grows in thickness and imperviousness—that reality which there is grave danger we might die without ever having known and yet which is simply our life, life as it really is, life disclosed at last and made clear, consequently the only life that is really lived, that life which in one sense is to be found at every moment in every man, as well as in the artist. But men fail to see it because they do not try to get light on it. And thus the past is encumbered with countless photographic negatives which lie there useless because the intelligence has not developed them.

In *Remembrance of Things Past* Proust does get his light on life as it really is. His strobelights pass and re-pass years, people, images, events, feelings, ideas, until they pierce that "formal knowledge," that "imperviousness." The passage just quoted appears toward the end of the book and the insight gained at this late stage has been developing, like a photographic negative, over the years and the seven books that compose *Remembrance of Things Past*. It comes to light first in *Swann's Way* in the magic lantern slides which the sleepless child casts on the wall of his bedroom. This child, who will grow old, is the fictitious autobiographical narrator.

Proust's use of such a narrator is daring and precarious. I certainly have no intention of going into all the subtleties. But a few points. The narrator is so like Proust in so many ways it is tempting to identify the two completely. Sensitive, emotionally dependent, neurasthenic, asthmatic, intelligent, rich. We are seduced further by the gradual identification of the "I" of the novel by the initial "M." Later in the book, as if weary of the game, the author seems to let down his guard and calls him Marcel. But whereas the narrator would like to be a writer, Proust is one, at least by the time he is writing his great work. The device is ironic and distancing but also turns back on itself to simulate the authentic, the subjective, the non-fictive. The force of the irony, however, resides in that major difference between the author and his almost double. Proust *is* actually writing. His narrator merely hopes to write. He is a procrastinator. He puts off the labour of creation, puts off his novel about time and memory. Now and then he takes up his pen, rededicates himself to the great task, sighs, writes a letter, and vegetates for a week.

Dedication, relapse, rededication, the pattern of procrastination is not accidental. Proust is saying something important about the nature of time and memory and the way a work of art develops. The artist must totally possess his subject, even if it has to be cycled and recycled through years of apparent meaninglessness. The psychic alarm clock has its own tick and its own tock. It will go off—in its own sweet time. Proust's narrator reaches this stage, we are led to believe, in old age when Proust's masterpiece abruptly ends. The life of the child who begins the book has come almost full circle. A mystic radiance finally reveals to an old man the meaning of his subject. We are led to believe the laziness of laziness, the habit of habit have borne fruit. Now the labour of labour must begin. If we close the book with a small doubting smile, it is only because we have come to know Proust's narrator very well, his ways and means. He has disclosed himself. Proust has seen to that. But I don't like to keep calling this charming, sickly, gifted creature the narrator. At the risk of some confusion, I will call him Marcel.

> I knew that when they were at table I should not be permitted to stay there for the whole of dinner-time, and that Mamma, for fear of annoying my father, would not allow me to give her in public the series of kisses that she would have had in my room. And so I promised myself that in the dining-room, as they began to eat and drink and as I felt the hour approach, I would put beforehand into this kiss, which was bound to be so brief and stealthy in execution, everything that my own efforts could put into it: would look out very carefully first the exact spot on her cheek where I would imprint it, and would so prepare my thoughts that I might be able, thanks to these mental preliminaries, to consecrate the whole of the minute Mamma would allow me to the sensation of her cheek against my lips. . . .

The child, who passionately longs for his mother's kiss and the sleep it brings, will become the adolescent, the young man, and the aging one who awaits the kiss of women and the kiss of redemptive vision. That vision will have to wait until the vicious circle of frustrated loves bodies forth a universal truth. Bed, women, kiss, touch, security, become an associative anodyne for this insomniac. But, like all good masochists, he will seem to invite the refusal of such bliss, and the anxiety which takes its place will become the necessary antecedent to pleasure. This involutional pattern ensures his role as victim, as lover rather than beloved, in the theatre and drama of his life where women star and where he, poor thing, can only suffer or pleasure under the changes of their mysterious light.

His difficult task of loving begins in childhood with the pinkly freckled Gilberte among pink hawthorns, proceeds at a more mature stage to the Duchesse de Guermantes, that heraldic figure in his imagination, and finds its apotheosis in the sweet cheat Albertine. The cast changes. The plot does not. It only thickens. But Marcel abstracts a general law:

> I had suffered much for Gilberte, for Mme. de Guermantes, and for

Albertine in succession. Successively too I had forgotten them, and only my love itself, addressed to, bestowed on different beings, had been enduring.

And is that all? All said and done? No.

If we do not love solely a Gilberte, then what made us suffer so keenly was not that we loved also an Albertine, but that our love is a portion of our soul which, regardless of the useful suffering this may cause us, must detach itself from its human objects in order to make clear to us and restore its quality of generality and give this love, an understanding of this love, to all the world, to the universal intelligence, and not first to this woman then to that, in whom this one and that of our successive selves seek to lose their identity,

It is distressing not to be able to give you more of the flesh and flowers, colours, gestures, intonations, the scent of the characters Proust creates in *Remembrance of Things Past*. But he is a discursive writer of the greatest subtlety and delicacy. I must be brief and a little brutal. What I'm trying to do in this discussion of Proust's cyclic notions is show his concern with men and money, groups and nations, as time engulfs and changes them. The social fabric of the novel is rich in classes, races, types, and individuals, all distinct but related to the total design. At the centre, fading but with colours still vivid enough to enchant and explore, is the aristocracy of France. And, in particular, one family. The Guermantes, with its many off-shoots, dominate the fantasies of Marcel in childhood, become real for him as he gravitates into their circle of affection, and gradually bore him. Here they are—viewed as an entity, not by the romantic child, but by the realistic, not yet disillusioned Marcel. He shows some promise for a would-be novelist:

The physical flexibility essential to the Guermantes was twofold; thanks to one of its forms, constantly in action, at any moment and if, for example, a male Guermantes were about to salute a lady, he produced a silhouette of himself made from the unstable equilibrium of a series of asymmetrical movements with nervous compensations, one leg dragging a little, either on purpose or because, having been broken so often in the hunting-field, it imparted to his trunk in its effort to keep pace with the other a deviation to which the upward thrust of one shoulder gave a counterpoise, while the monocle settled itself before his eye, raising an eyebrow just as the tuft of hair on the forehead was lowered in the formal bow; the other flexibility, like the form of the wave, the wind or the ocean track which is preserved on the shell or the vessel, was so to speak stereotyped in a sort of fixed mobility, curving the arched nose which, beneath the blue, protruding eyes, above the over-thin lips, from which, in the women, there emerged a raucous voice, recalled the fabulous origin attributed in the sixteenth century by the complaisance of parasitic and Hellenising genealogists to his race, ancient beyond dispute, but not to the degree of antiquity which they claimed when they gave as its source the mythological impregnation of a nymph by a divine Bird.

The range of Proust's imagination shown in that single sentence is stunning. He is a literary evolutionist, as precise a researcher as Darwin, almost scientifically detached, unfolding time and its works with patient care. Key words and concepts recur to forward the evolutionary idea. He speaks of decades, generations, cycles of twenty years, epochs. The process of metamorphosis, so frequently invoked, and the image of the chrysalis can refer to an individual soul, a social or historic event, or an idea. He dwells on genealogies; on methods of plant reproduction; on cell regeneration; on chemical changes of state. Words are rolled back to root meanings in long passages on etymology; as cosmologist, he will send a star to its dying end or bring a new planet into our orbit. Evolutionist. Unfolder. His range of vision captures not only the human comedy with inspired exactitude, but the larger motions of nature and cosmos which ensure the tone of the relativist.

He sees danger in simple recurrence—in wars or the inbreeding of the aristocracy, for instance, and Proust loses no time in having Marcel make friends with the elegant young army officer, St.-Loup, a member of the Guermantes family, to move onto the subject of military history, like a little boy with his toy soldiers suggesting a theory of history. At

Doncières, where St.-Loup is billeted, Marcel listens as the men discuss strategy. St.-Loup, whose homosexuality symbolizes the dying aristocracy, and who will be killed in World War I, is enthusiastic:

> Battles like Ulm, Leipzig, Cannae. I can't say whether there is ever going to be another war, or what nations are going to fight in it, but if war does come, you may be sure that it will include (and deliberately on the commander's part) a Cannae, an Austerlitz, a Rosbach, a Waterloo. Some of our people say quite openly that Marshall von Schieffer and General Falkenhausen have prepared a Battle of Cannae against France, in the Hannibal style . . . it's no more obsolete than the *Iliad*.

"But," Marcel asks, "does the genius of the commander count for nothing?" And a long discussion ensues. As historian, Proust is less impressive than as psychologist or sociologist. But he is a novelist who transforms his researches into art. The associative patterns of images and themes, the cross-fertilizing or auto-fecundating, in and out of season, of his many characters, the imitative designs passion and history create, the complex musical development of the novel itself produce a formal beauty, the grandeur of art. The sweep of his time is graceful and leisurely, but in fact time passes, through *Swann's Way* to the final book, *The Past Recaptured*, with increasing swiftness. Communications speed up between his characters—all those aristocratic friends and lovers, *le tout Paris*, and those diplomats, artists, actresses, army officers, dilettantes, parasites, servants (which I've had to by-pass so cruelly), whether they be in Combray, Balbec, Paris, Doncières, or Venice. Technology hastens the social meld. In the beginning, messages are delivered by hand; then little blue envelopes shuttle through the pneumatic. First, carriages stop at the hotel at Balbec, then motor cars make spectacular arrivals. Emotional and actual territories are covered at greater speeds. Lovers may still write letters; now they may also telephone, and the circuits connect with increasing efficiency. Marcel watches "aeroplanes" with fascinated apprehension, as if they came flying out of some prophetic bestiary. The First World War comes, bombs fall from the air; millions meet brief death. Fashions change more rapidly, but, as Mme. de Guermantes says, "All the old styles come back in dress and music and painting." The five major salons of the novel, those planetary centres of attraction dominated by their very French and luminous hostesses, retain many of the old faces, but new ones appear. The social ladder is a busy place, hard to climb, easy to fall from. Marriages and love affairs cross class boundaries. Political passions undulate and storm up to break old ties and bind new ones. And history, that great cloud of unknowing, shaping, reshaping the now larger and faster-moving destinies of nations, until time, it seems, must have a stop. Or at least a breathing spell:

> The new sanitarium to which I retired at that time did not cure me any more than had the first and a long time elapsed before I left it. During the railway journey back to Paris, I fell to thinking of my lack of literary talent which I had early suspected along the Guermantes way. . . .

The same old Marcel returning? Not knowing his psychic alarm clock will sound. Not knowing it won't tell time. Something quite other does that. I have not been able to detail the sensory images that become emblematic in the inner life of the narrator and accrete meaning in the course of *Remembrance of Things Past*. But now they are to emerge in their fullness. Marcel does not seek; he finds. The "*recherche*" ends; quest is rewarded by vision. He stumbles on the truth:

> Engrossed in unhappy meditations, I had entered the court of the Guermantes residence and, in my absorption, failed to notice an automobile that was coming in; at the chauffeur's cry I had barely time to get out of the way and, in stepping back, struck my foot against some unevenly cut flagstones leading to a carriage house. In recovering my balance, I put my foot on a stone that was a little lower than the one next to it; immediately all my discouragement vanished before a feeling of happiness which I had experienced at different moments of my life, at the sight of trees I thought I recognized when driving around Balbec, or the church spires of Martinville, or the savour of a *madeleine*, dipped in herb tea, or from many other sensations I have mentioned, which had seemed to me

13

to be synthesized in the last works of Vinteuil. . . . The feeling of happiness which had just come over me was, indeed, exactly the same as I had experienced while eating the *madeleine*, but at that time I put off seeking the deep-lying causes for it. There was a purely material difference in the mental images evoked. A deep azure blue intoxicated my sight, impressions of coolness and dazzling light hovered near me and, in my eagerness to seize them, not daring to move— I stood there, swaying back and forth, as I had done a moment before, one foot on the higher stone, and the other on the lower, indifferent to the possible amusement of the large crowd of chauffeurs. Each time that I merely repeated the action physically, the effort was in vain; but if I forgot the Guermantes' reception and succeeded in recapturing the sensation I had felt the instant I placed my feet in that position, again the dazzling elusive vision brushed me with its wings, as if to say, "Seize me in my flight, if you have the power, and try to solve the riddle of happiness I propound to you."

It is the beginning of the famous, climactic meditation on the nature of time, memory, and reality. The past recaptured. It does not speak of hours and days. Something quite other does that. Returning to society after a long absence, to the salon of the Princesse de Guermantes, Marcel, fresh from his radiant vision, enters. A grotesque sight meets his unclouded eyes:

The first instant I did not understand why I could not immediately recognize the master of the house and the guests, who seemed to have "made themselves up," usually with powdered hair, in a way that completely changed their appearance. The Prince, as he received his guests still retained the genial manner of a fairyland king which had struck me in him the first time, but this day, having apparently submitted to the same etiquette as he had established for his guests, he had rigged himself up with a white beard and what looked like leaden soles which made his feet drag heavily. He seemed to have taken it upon himself to represent the Seven Stages of Man.

All the guests seem to "have rigged themselves up" as for a masquerade.

And successfully. Marcel is puzzled. Gradually he discerns beneath the changes of time features which identify people he has long known. And slowly they puzzle out who he is, or try to find in his "present appearance some different recollection of the past." The sudden aging of our first-person narrator comes as a shock, and the caricature of the other human subjects of time is painful. Death is in the wings. Self and subjectivity intensify. But the vision brushes with its wings, as if to say, "Seize me in my flight."

> And then, as maskers in their masks are shown
> Different of feature, if they cast aside
> The assumed appearance that was not their own
> So into festal aspect glorified
> Sparkles and flowers changed: both Heaven's courts I saw
> Revealed before me opening far and wide.
> O, splendour of God, by whose largess I saw
> With mine eyes truth realmed in triumph fill
> My lips with power to re-tell how I saw.

Dante. *The Divine Comedy.* The "Paradiso." The multifoliate Rose of Paradise. Where have we been in *A La Recherche du Temps Perdu?* In hell, purgatory, paradise? We have been in a human comedy, certainly, not a divine one, and with human love and human hope. With Proust and Marcel we have joined in the search for "that reality which there is grave danger we might die without ever having known and yet which is simply our life." As the sentences turn upon themselves, as images occur and recur, as the life cycles of Proust's characters complete themselves in corruption, in beauty, in wisdom, in aging—rings of trees telling time, waterlilies petalling and unpetalling—Proust moves slowly, engaging, disengaging his themes and variations on the human comedy brushed with the vision of the divine. *Remembrance of Things Past* is a breathtaking achievement of rhythmic movement and contrapuntal effects, manoeuvering neurosis, social class, and statecraft into images of fate, history, and myth, seizing us in our flight with "that reality . . . which is simply our life."

And now I'll take you back along the Guermantes way, dark wood, purgatory, paradise of the inner life, where as a child Marcel walked, enchanted child, visionary artist:

Presently the course of the Vivonne became choked with water-plants. At first they appeared singly, a lily, for instance, which the current across whose path it had unfortunately grown, would never leave at rest for a moment, so that, like a ferry boat mechanically propelled, it would drift over to one bank only to return to the other, eternally repeating its double journey. Thrust towards the bank, its stalk would be straightened out, lengthened, strained almost to break-ing point until the current again caught it, its green moorings swung back over their anchorage and brought the unhappy plant to what might fitly be called its starting point, since it was fated not to rest there a moment before moving off once again. I would still find it there, on one walk after another, always in the same helpless state, suggesting certain victims of neurasthenia, among whom my grand-father would have included my aunt Léonie, who present without modification, year after year, the spectacle of their odd and unac-countable habits, which they always retain to the end; caught in the treadmill of their own maladies and eccentricities, their futile en-deavours to escape serve only to actuate its mechanism, to keep in motion the clockwork of their strange, ineluctable, fatal daily round. Such as these was the water-lily, and also like one of those wretches whose peculiar torments, repeated indefinitely throughout eternity, aroused the curiosity of Dante, who would have inquired of them at greater length and in fuller detail from the victims themselves, had not Virgil, striding on ahead, obliged him to hasten after him at full speed, as I must hasten after my parents.

But farther on the current slackened where the stream ran through a property thrown open to the public by its owner, who had made a hobby of aquatic gardening, so that the little ponds into which the Vivonne was here diverted were a-flower with water-lilies. As the banks at this point were thickly wooded, the heavy shade of the trees gave the water a background which was ordinarily dark green, although sometimes, when we were coming home on a calm evening after a stormy afternoon, I have seen in its depths a clear, crude blue that was almost violet, suggesting a floor of Japanese cloisonné. Here and there, on the surface, floated, blushing like a strawberry, the scarlet heart of a lily set in a ring of white petals.

•ᴗ

On one of my walks along the beach I unexpectedly came across a huge boulder, a face carved in its stone. Strong, mysterious, primitive, ovoid. I stared at it; it stared back from a time that could not be remembered, could only be imagined. Proust, who had emerged from his cork-lined room for a stroll along the beach, was beside me. "Imagine that," I said. "Well, imagine *that*," he said.

1970, REVISED IN 1982

Letter
by Gary Geddes

Dear Phyllis:

I'm looking forward to doing the interview with you, by mail *and* in person hopefully. It will help me formulate my own ideas too on the subject of the line. I think Levertov is right about the importance of the line, but less reliable on the absolute weight in terms of timing that it has. I'd say the weight of an end-line is very relative, depending almost entirely on context, the degree of syntactical activity (syntactivity?) and the momentum of sound and idea to hit the bearing-point of each line. Does a comma plus an end-line therefore equal 1 1/2 commas? If so, what is the real duration of the comma—it all depends on the kind of noise, the buzz, each poem makes.

And the stanza. Lord, how to prescribe for its usage. Does the stanza have to be self-contained, with a closure either given by way of a full-stop or implied by spacing? Obviously not. Good poems break that convention often. And a comma hanging at the end of a stanza, what does that do, beyond keeping those words from sliding into the abyss that follows?

I wish Levertov would tell us more clearly how the line can be best used and then show how that method has been/must be broken to avoid tedium or predictability. I, for example, often separate the noun and adjective, precisely in order to *avoid* the sense of closure, of finality, or predictability that one associates with the phrasally determined line. The pause in many cases, then, is mainly eliminated or only hinted at. The advantage lies, I believe, in a subtle increase in energy and meaning that comes from making the noun and its qualifier appear separated in space but linked in time, thus giving a three-way focus on two words.

So I doubt if Levertov's theory of the line is any more reliable than Olson's breath-unit theory. We need, perhaps, to come at it via Olson, since one man's 4/4 time is another's 2/2 time, and then try to show how the material, the subject itself, calls up a certain momentum, as a lover does to one's pulse and breathing habits; this is where the question of tradition begins to get interesting, because one can see certain poets gaining strength by working against the iambic pentametre line with syllabics or some other mode of measuring.

Your own poem "Poetics Against the Angel of Death" moves out onto the wide prairie in the last line, as a spatial pun and a manifesto, and in so doing it sits in the tradition of the free twentieth and the more ordered eighteenth centuries. Pope could make the line crawl or leap or dance by virtue of this clever use of punctuation and syntax, so that the end of the line was less important than the main portion. Is that too Aristotelian—happiness of the line is more important—no, the means towards the end of the line is more important than the end itself? I want you "to put yourself on the line" and say *what a line can't do without*, i.e., something for the ear, eye or mind, preferably all three.

That's all for now. Please drop me a *line* as you feel, the urge. . . .

All the best

Gary

1981

On the Line

To whom am I talking? The awkward sound of that "to whom." Am I talking? No. My mouth is shut. Gary's letter arrives; I feel oppressed. It's Gary who wants the answers, though I put him up to it. Why did I start this dialogue which I now rebel against? On the poetic line. Let me discover the reasons for that as I try to find out to whom I am talking.

Last night, feeling uneasy, I turned again to Adrienne Rich, rereading her essays, "The Tensions of Anne Bradstreet" and "When We Dead Awaken: Writing as Re-Vision." I think I am trying to re-vision the approach to the line and all such matters. Gary, in Montreal, during that discussion we didn't tape, gave me the lead, talking about shorelines, tidelines. And Doug Barbour before that with his title *Shore Lines*. Sure Lines.

I look again at the yellow dying tulip on the table. It is stretched out on an almost true horizontal. The flower has sliced itself exactly in half. I sympathize. The half tulip, halved tulip, hangs exposed. I was not there to hear the petals fall. They form a curve of yellow on the glass tabletop; they dropped to form a new line, a waxy curvature, unique to the forces that befell them. *Curvature.*

That is what I am coming to, the physics of the poem. Energy/Mass. Waxy splendour, the massive quiet of the fallen tulip petals. So much depends upon: the wit of the syntax, the rhythm and speed of the fall, the drop, the assumption of a specific light, curved.

The oppression lifts as I draw the line on the page like this

---

A hair-line, a hair's breadth. The wind in the willow. Hair's breath. Talking to myself on an April afternoon, my birth-day. The opening of that crack, of Duncan's field ("a wild field," he says, "I'm sort of interested in wild feelings, wild thoughts—and I don't mean like whoopee—but like wild life"). Or "a series of fields folded." Today, the fifty-fourth, the flowers arrive: roses, daisies, carnations, tulips (red), grape hyacinth, dead daffodils. Are falling into line, each one its own line, of its own accord, curved. Is that what we seek in sky, in field, in poem—*curvature?*

• ⤳

Enjambment: As bad as "to whom." Ugly, stupid, door-jamb. For closing. Foreclosing. Squashed.

• ⤳

The short line is "for candor," says Duncan. Or terror, say I. Notes Toward a Poetics of Terror. Pull down thy vanity. The tulip is moving horizontally towards the light (tropos), cells burning brightly, dying out. Snuff out the poem. Stuff it. ("For flowers are peculiarly the poetry of Christ"— Christopher Smart.)

• ⤳

Syntactivity. Under the electron microscope. Oh look and see. Against this, an image pushes through of splicing tape. Janet in the listening room late at night at CBC. Listening room, the poem as listening room. Cut twenty seconds. Hear how they sound! Glossy plastic ribbon on the cutting room floor. Curling.

Ribbon at the end of the race. Break it. Ribbon at ceremonial opening of the bridge. Cut it with big authorial scissors. Champagne all around.

I am out of it. Cut. Splice. Play it again. To whom am I talking? Seriously. A fine line.

"The line has shattered," Olson gasped in that interview I did with him in 1963.

The water is boiling. Kenneth Koch's poem, "The Boiling Water." The seriousness of the boiling point for the water. For the tea, for me. The syntactivity (Geddes). So Gary forces me to this ebullience. The dance of the intellect in the syllable, for Olson. Knuckles of the articulate hand.

• ⤳

Certainties: that the long line (in English) is aggressive, with much "voice." Assertive, at least. It comes from assurance (or hysteria), high tide, full moon, open mouth, big-mouthed Whitman, yawp, yawp, and Ginsberg— howling. Male.

Modulations. Now take Kit Smart in *Jubilate Agno*. Yes, sure of himself, madly hurting. Sore lines. "Silly Fellow, Silly Fellow." Blessed. Based on Hebraic long-line psalmistry. (The short line, *au contraire*, private palmistry, heart line, cut to the quick.) Gary, forget the commas, line breaks, caesura (plucked from the womb, untimely), the modes of measuring (though you are right about Levertov's one-half comma as frivolous), and look again at that idea: Behold, I am here. Even as the leaves of grass. Sexton *imitates* Smart (Behold, I am *almost* here). She was not able to walk that line alone. Few women are, but they are learning. Anne, you took Christopher right into the poem for company.

In "For Fyodor," the beetle is aggressive, enraged, monologuing dramatically along the extended line. Poor Fyodor, foaming at the mouth, harangued by this Trickster (yells and chuckles): "You are mine, Dostoevsky." Big-mouthed, proletarian, revolting beetle. The balance of power unbalanced. (See also Wayman's industrial poems.) Notes from the Insect Underground. Spider Webb.

• ◞

Notes. The musical phrase, go with it, sd. Pound. Another big mouth, or was it really a big ear, delicate as seashell or tulip cup? He changed our borders, changed the shape of the poem, its energy potential, for the "data grid"? (Ed Sanders) And presented us with the freedom we now mediate. Who are "we"? To whom, etc.? Emily?

• ◞

—Emily—those gasps, those inarticulate dashes—those incitements—hiding what unspeakable—foul breath? But not revolting; *subversive.* Female. Hiding yourself—Emily—no, compressing yourself, even singing yourself—tinily—with compacted passion—a violet storm—

• ◞

Compare:

Now you are sitting doubled up in pain.
What's that for?

Doubled up I feel
small like these poems
the area of attack
is diminished.

I did not count the syllables or the ways. A hare's breath.

• ⌐

Sidelines. I play by ear. And the eye. The yellow tulip stretched on its stem, petals falling, a new moon, a phase.

I drink the tea. The seriousness of the moving line, for me. Detritus, the phenomenal world in Kenneth Koch. He cannot pull the wool over his eyes. Giving up on the weights and measures of the fine line to *hear* the water boiling, to overhear himself. Am I talking? Almost, to K.K. He lays himself bare in anxiety. Kroetsch sees anxiety as central to the short-lined *Naked Poems*—and the post-modern long poem generally. But the long-lined unyawping K.K. (unaggressive, relatively, unhysterical, relatively) fields his anxiety as you sprawl on your carpet, Kenneth, sprawl on the page, talking to me!

Comedian that he is, he throws away his lines. Hooray.

Hook, line, and sinker.

• ⌐

Sound poetry. "Open wide," says doctor as he/she depresses your tongue to look down the little red lane.

From whence comes the dragon! Or the Four Horsemen. Whee. Whoa. Woe. Stop. Or that horse-thief Rothenberg. Technicians of the Sacred on the firing line.

But *no lines now.* Notes only. Notation. "A new alphabet gasps for air"

Actually, an old alphabet

Shamanic

The Gutenberg Galaxy self-destructing under my hand and—

the mystical numbers come through the mail from Gwendolyn MacEwen, April 7, 1981:

23

1 - The Bond
3 - Divine Interception
5 - Impending Doom
7 - Weakness

"To control reality" when she was a child. Holding the line. The oppression of all that for the wild child.

Verse as numbers. Mystical systems. Music of the spheres. Curvature. Curlicue. Of the tulip of

Heraclitean fire.

"I am learning to be / a poet, caught in the / Divine Storm" (Bowering, "The Breath, Release").

•ﾉ

Poundsound. Prosody: The articulation of the total sound of the poem. Or of the tulip, the yellow tulip, P.K.'s "squeaky" flower.

•ﾉ

And ultimately meaning, as you say, Gary, the movement of the meaning, the syntactivity, radioactivity, power.

When we dead arise.

I once complained about Adrienne Rich's line breaks, but when I read *The Dream of a Common Language*, I felt shame, shame, ashamed, that I had ever been so petty, knowing that, like Marie Curie, your wounds, Adrienne, and your power come from the same source.

•ﾉ

I talk like this only to myself with my mouth shut. Laying it on the line.

EDMONTON APRIL 8/9, 1981

Up the Ladder:
Notes on the Creative
Process

Where do poems come from? That is a continuing mystery unfolding itself with each new poem but never thoroughly disclosing itself. Does story or event precede poem? Does the reader or listener have to know details of event or story in order to understand the poem completely? Or does knowing the plot simply make the event of the poem itself more gossipy, more humane, less autocratic? I raise such questions because poets are so frequently asked how their poems come about. For poems do "come about" in roundabout ways, hanging around as moods (silent, morose, dumbfounded, blank, or high, floaty flights of ideas, constellated); as dreams (technicolour nightmares, nightfoals, nightfools); as dreary tasks of dailiness, as knotted relationships, as passion.

I buy an old house and begin to paint—coats and coats of white. (First draft, second draft, third?) The *living-room* first. I shall transform it from tacky darkness into light. The mind is free to obsess with the repetitive movements, the rhythm of the task. The slight toxification from the paint gives me strange ideas: why didn't I take the money and run? To travel, to see real paintings, change my life, bloom upon the world? Here I am only changing a house, an investment for my older age. The money for this place has come from the sale of my last house, which I had also painted and papered and fixed up. Occupational therapy. I am in the corner of the room now, the last corner, the last draft, cornering myself with . . . why didn't I take the money and run? I am up the ladder (Jacob's), reaching toward the ceiling, remembering how we had painted his house, a Saturday afternoon, the Metropolitan Opera on the radio, the tension between us, covering up. A cover.

Now this house, mine, the old house. I want to put something down. The paint brush. I come down the ladder, go to my study, get a writing pad, begin to write, back against a wall, knees up for writing. The ache of that other house, the cottage on the lake, in my bones, but the words flow easily:

Painting the Old House

It carries me over
stroke by stroke
my Bourgeois affiliations
the bad spots
of the guilty body
the walls
covered recovered
in the blank of absences
the blot the stained
character of knowing
the cat's claws clicking
over the linoleum
telling me she is hungry.
So am I. We eat
the body of knowledge
the Pamper tuna
the carrot's sweet orange
we bite with aging teeth
in between strokes—here
fear is all that was desire
abandoned, thought of
thought out today
in the white paint
covering recovering.
I would cry if I could
I would unwrap my
wounds to show you how
it is up here on the
ladder where it's
warm. I would call

you again and again
out of our painting
ourselves into a corner
where you would not let me
turn around to see
what, where all that
stammer, shifty gaze
of panic over the colour
of trim for the fireplace
the mantel. Afterwards
the scalpels of our benefactors
sending us back to
old time restorations
the balanced diet, exercise
repression—all that
I am painting over and over
white . . .

Etcetera. This is what at Banff is known as "free fall" and does not refer to sky diving, though it is a plunge. Into murk, unconscious psychological disclosures, grammatical errors—I don't eat cat food and my cat does not chew carrots. Finger poetry. Shit. But a line, lines suddenly with the rattle of poem:

what, where all that
stammer, shifty gaze
of panic . . .

Your choice might be different, perhaps

the cat's claws clicking
over the linoleum . . .

The free fall ends like this:
                                        this
white cold interior

I have administered for your
sake, for God's sake, for the state's sake
for the mistaken mirrors
of anyone who dares
to look here.

Maybe? No matter. What interests me most here is the abundance of
guilt expressed and the accuracy of most of the line-breaks achieved in
the rush. I put it aside, cross to my desk and take a postcard of a Vasarely
painting called *Tridim-C*, painted in 1968. I look at it briefly. All that
year I had been receiving Vasarely cards from two separately travelling
friends. I had looked at them often and had even used them in a First
Year Creative Writing drama class as ideas for stage sets and examples of
shifting perspectives. The poem begins to emerge from under the layers
of paint, under the layers of guilt, of repression, into the codes of play,
trance and language.

The paintings of Vasarely
on postcards coming
through the mail
from Aix-en-Provence
from Detroit and Tallahassee
Fla. Fla. a cube a
cube a fla-sound op-
ening on to an *étage*
et age . . .

Obviously, I am not into the poem yet, being too mindful, yet the *play* is
already there and will emerge as a main element of the poem. The French,
which will insist on being present, has also arrived. After one page of
darts and bull's-eyes, I find the pace and the poem really begins, becoming eventually:

Vasarely
Vasarely arrives through the mail
disguised as a postcard from Aix-en-

Provence, Detroit, or Tallahassee, Fla.
He is hiding his secret vice in a cube
of mauve.

I am wrong. Vasarely is a red telephone box.
No. Vasarely is in a telephone box (blue).
He is dialing Tridim-C 1968 — *Allo! Allo!*
He connects with Tallahassee and Saturday's
death in the afternoon opera.
Pourquoi es-tu si triste, ma chère?
He is death in the afternoon.

Vasarely is no longer in his green telephone box.
He is in Sri Lanka standing on his head.
He sticks out his tongue and wriggles
his fingers in his ears.
He hates Wagner. He disappears.

He is, perhaps, an opening on
the invisible — *Allo . . . Allo . . .*

He dials again (in his index finger
the fingerprints of Mars):
"Tu es dégoutante, ma soeur!
You are the one I blame." He hangs
up smiling.
I myself have brown eyes.

I shift my gaze from the abode of adoration.

Ach! He is a grey gnome in a playpen
dribbling integers crying
for the holy spectrum
I would freeze him into a tray of ice-cubes
but he'd only look out at me
with his aqua eyes.

He's out and scuttling around the corner
pressing among the archangels and their
sibling rivals — *Allo . . . Allo . . .*
dicing for multiples of eleven.

(*Pourquoi es-tu si triste?*)

He is withdrawn again into the
Everlasting, studying his *Book of
Changes*, his horrendous hexagrams.
He is laughing and laughing.

And only yesterday I thought I saw
him painting himself into a corner.
(Ochre). He caught me looking.
He hopped up the ladder
and then he came down.
He fanned a pack of red.
It laid me low. It said:

"*Pourquoi es-tu si triste, chérie?
C'est toujours moi.
C'est moi. C'est Vasarely.*"

The preoccupations of painting the old house are transformed surprisingly to reveal a poem partly about sibling rivalry, partly about the perverse, sadistic, gamelike and revelatory nature of the artist (and poet).
That Hitler was a house painter and paperhanger and a would-be artist
had, of course, passed through my head as I stood on that ladder painting myself into a poem.

When the revolution began in Iran in January 1979, I was fascinated by the leisurely pace of the Shah's exit and was listening to
newscasts with attention. On the evening of January 16 CBC's "The World
at Six" began, "The King of Kings leaves the Peacock Throne." I was
startled by the unusually dramatic turn the CBC news had taken off on. I
was cooking dinner and stopped to write that line down. A great line, I

thought, though I would "improve" it by changing it to "The King of Kings has left the Peacock Throne," a perfect iambic pentameter, that "Hound of Heaven in our stress," as I've said elsewhere, which I usually try to avoid. At the time I was teaching Creative Writing at the University of Victoria and had been talking about the villanelle, since some of the students were interested in hearing about traditional forms. Or perhaps I had simply dared to raise the subject. Anyhow, the form was on my mind. I wanted to do something immediately with that line and I thought it would be perfect in a villanelle with its two repeated lines and rhymes. The same newscast announced that the Shah would probably go to Los Angeles. He never did, but that idea became the other refrain line of the poem: "The Shah will make the Yankee sun his own." I have never, until now, published the poem, though I did send it to *Saturday Night* in the high of completion. Fortunately it was returned and I filed it away.

"The King of Kings has left the Peacock Throne"
CBC RADIO NEWS, JANUARY 16/79

The King of Kings has left the Peacock Throne,
a langorous, long, courtly getaway.
The Shah will make the Yankee sun his own.

You heard the quake kick up God's sticks and stones?
A January omen, would you say?
The King of Kings has left the Peacock Throne.

The cars are honking in the streets of bone.
The people dance and kiss a different way.
The Shah will make the Yankee sun his own.

The ones who died street-fighting would have known
that Allah chose Iran and not L.A.
The King of Kings has left the Peacock Throne.

Oh Persian oil and flesh and foreign loans,

Oh jewelled and Swiss accounted disarray.
The Shah will make the Yankee sun his own.

And now Khomeini comes to say he's won,
But where is Rolof Beny and his camera — eh?
The King of Kings has left the Peacock Throne.
The Shah will make the Yankee sun his own.

The villanelle is one of the forms that Robin Skelton calls "obsessive." But obsessions are not always so neat and tidy. The light is mauve. The light is mauve. The light is mauve. Obsessions are vital to the creative process, a stalling often, a signalling, a belligerent mental tic. Mine are frequently related to various physiological states. The light is mauve. At that time my thyroid was dying, though I thought I was. The light is mauve. For several days that line haunted me. I began one poem with it. I began another. They weren't right. I didn't know what the line meant. Then I had the dream. A riderless horse, wild, was running down Morningside Road where I live. Passing the lilac hedge, it bounded through and crashed up the garden, galloped behind the house. There's still some life in the old girl yet, I thought. *Nightmare*. But the horse, I was sure, was a stallion: the Shadow, the Other, animus, unbridled passion. (The punning aspect of dreams has particular charm and use for the poet.) Or Father. Father and horses. Yes, that was it; it was both. The light is mauve is death. Dead Father. And fatherly things began coming back to me, the pictures on his wall, his obsession with horses, his pride in his riding skills, he himself something of a horse in profile. His marvellous smile. The light.

Father

The light is mauve
my eye's iris blooms
into the nightmare of
riderless horse, the sleep honey
sings through the lilac
and I smell ash.

I touch the skin of the
horse, his pelt, thinking
of Father's military ride
Father's pomaded hair brushed
back, brown, and his long beautiful
hands holding the reins
just so, horse dancing.
And at the end, Father
smiling his great Rosicrucian smile
sniffing the light
flicked whip of lilac
his eyes seeing behind me
the Rosy Cross.

It seems almost banal these days to talk about dreams and poems, but in dreams reside much of that mystery I spoke of earlier. Sometimes the dream guides me, as in "Lines from Gwen. Lines for Ben," where the dream and poem seem to be saying, among other things, something about identity and vocation. In that poem the dream material comes untransformed into the poem. The structure of dreams can teach us something about form, even about tone, and both these matters became part of the problem and then the solution of "Composed Like Them," where the dream content mixed the comic and the sublime. It is easy to become solemn and self-serious about this subject, but the sheer entertainment of many of my dreams should keep me out of harm's way.

But can I go deeper? I see that I do not want either to disclose to you or reveal to myself the darker territory inhabited by the Creator Spirit. Reticence. Is only "story" permissible in these confessional notes? The rest sealed, hermetic, a barrier I cannot pass? I ask myself, is what lies behind the barrier embedded in the *structure* of what I have written so far in this essay rather than in the overt content? Structure as substance, as subtext. Why did I choose the episode of the old house—why *that* episode—to begin talking about where poems come from? Is the fact that I am now finally painting the exterior of the house the reason, or is it just that the "Vasarely" story is one of my better anecdotes? The old house led to the Trickster nature of the artist, with an aside here about Hitler. Onto the Shah of Iran through obvious associations, to revolution and the villanelle. The villanelle took me to obsession, dream and death. Repression / Resistance; Tradition / Revolt. Death. The old versus the new: Transformations. Creator Spirit as transformational guardian. Is that what I'm talking about beyond the chatter? Or is resistance, in the psychoanalytic sense now, the actual subject coming about? Or is rebellion against the inner censor the more exact source of the poem? Perhaps I have discovered now the secret project of this essay and have taken myself beyond mere anecdote.

It occurs to me to ask if the drafts might also constitute sub-text, their prior existence giving the finished poem a more intense life, as if the complete poem contains layers of earlier incarnations hidden within it. In that case the poem which comes about through numerous drafts would have the intenser existence, in a Rilkean sense. But I really doubt this is so. Many of my best or most effective poems were written quickly, with only one or two drafts and a few minor corrections at the finish. "For Fyodor," which meets all the requirements of the dramatic monologue, was written swiftly with no conscious decisions being made about form, line-length, voice, etc. "Eschatology of Spring," a many-layered poem, took much more effort, the beginning of the poem being maddeningly resistant to the intent of the poem and having to do with Carson McCuller's indestructibility! The imperfections in "Imperfect Sestina" which begin to occur in the fourth stanza with the word "illumination" came about through speed of writing and the workings of the unconscious. I have learned to pay attention to so-called mistakes, and this one told me that "illumination" wanted to take over the poem. I therefore reinforced the mistake by repeating the word insistently, disrupting the compulsive sestina form with another compulsion which shed more light. "The Time of Man," inspired by a scientific essay and dealing with quite complex ideas, was composed easily and happily on a hot summer day in the sun (as was "Sitting" which is about sitting in the sun composing the self and the world). How such easy arrivals differ from "free fall" is a puzzle, but I'm sure the shaping and timing capacity of the unconscious must take most of the credit. Another poem inspired by a scientific work, a beautiful little book called *Field Guide to Snow Crystals*, took several months of dissatisfied doodling and then finally found its form.

Field Guide to Snow Crystals

      —stellar rime
  star crystals in a sunfield
  of snow. No
                two crystals exactly alike (like
  me and the double I've never known
              or the four-leaf clover)

      a down drifting
  of snow
        spatial dendrites
            irregular germs
  snow grows
      scales skeletons fernlike extensions
        needles scrolls
          and
        sheaths branches

lightly or *heavily*
      rimed
  stars on cold ground shining
        ice lattice!

For the field guides me/my
        flutterhand
  to a fistful of
      plates clusters minute columns
      Graupel-like snow of lump type
       solid and hollow bullets
        cup

  Cupped in my hand
      thrown across a field
  "or . . . a series of fields folded"
  a ball   star

("tiny columns and plates fallen from very cold air")
a quick curve into

        sky/my
             surprised

winterbreath
  a *snowflake*

     caught midway in your throat—

This poem which took such effort and many drafts to write is innocent enough, and yet I have just revised it again to release the left-hand margin and make a few other changes. The poem is about snow crystals, but it is also about the Field theory of poetry and so may not be quite as innocent as it appears. "The Days of the Unicorns" virtually wrote itself, or dreamed itself when I was once again unwell and lying down.

Lying down is part of my method of composition, being prone being close to sleep and dream. Throughout composition of this piece, for instance, I have lain down several times to allow the thoughts to shape themselves. Or I will wake from sleep to find a problem solved—or raised. This morning I woke at 3 A.M. and read through what I had written. I had gone to bed dissatisfied with the style and the superficiality of what had happened up to the story of "Father." By 6 A.M. I was beginning to see I needed to take a look at structure rather than style to find out what I was really talking about. The exercise has taken me this far and brought me through an impasse, if not through that hermetically sealed door.

Now I walk away from that door entirely to return to gossip. A strategic move.

A young woman in Edmonton comes to ask me for advice about her novel. She says she is a psychic, is taking courses on psychism or whatever. She has beautiful large eyes that see a great deal. I take her word and her eyes for it. We go and have coffee, talk for more than an hour. I want her to tell me about being a psychic, but she says another day today it's the novel. We come back to my office for more talk. Behind my desk I have tacked up a postcard (postcards seem to play an increasingly important role in my writing life, as do parentheses) of an Egyptian cat, a little sarcophagus in the Royal Ontario Museum. Stately, black with earrings! My psychic leaves, but immediately returns to ask, "Have you ever written about that cat?" I admit I have not. "You should," she says firmly, and I say, "All right, I will." A strange moment for me because I usually resist being told to do anything. I feel she knows more than I do and my intuition trusts her intuition.

The same afternoon I receive a letter from the Edmonton poet Ted Blodgett. We had had lunch a few days earlier to discuss his new book *Beast Gate*, which had perplexed me, though I went to lunch thinking I had triumphed in "breaking the code." The letter was a series of further comments on his poems, including one called "*Chat*." Two references to cats in a half day had to be a synchronous instruction and I began to write the poem that became "Messages."

Messages

"They are always projecting themselves.
Cats play to cats we cannot see.
This is confidential."
                    (LETTER FROM E.D. BLODGETT)
The young psychic comes back from halfway down the hall
to tell me to write about the cat on the postcard
tacked to the wall above my typewriter.

There is an understanding between us, and I show her
a photo in the *Journal* where the cat appears behind
my shoulder—

A piece of politics. A creature of state.

Out of Ptolemy's reign, cast in bronze (earrings restored)
far from Egypt now in its northern home.
Probable use: to hold the bones of a kitten.
Representative on this earth of the Goddess Bastet.

She prances toward me down the ramp of the poem
sent to me by the young psychic who is writing

an historical novel.
She moves toward me through an aura composed
of new light and the golden dust of Ptolemy,
Halfway down the ramp her high ears turn against
the task of the poem toward allurements
of stockmarket and monopoly.

Cats play to cats we cannot see.

Now it is night. I have locked her in this pyramid
of my own free will. She toys with the unwinding
sheet of a mummified king, paws at royal jewels
and sighs.
As I sleep at the 5 A.M. poem's edge she sniffs my skin
for news of her old lost world.
She names the Princes as they pass
heading for Bay Street in the winter blight.

They are always projecting themselves.
This is confidential.

Now it is morning in North Nineteen Hundred and Eighty.
The message clear: price of gold slumps.
War cracks at the border.
The Queen's cold mouth sends warning:

Beware.

How to get out of the poem without a scratch?
Each cast of the line seductive and minimal.
The ramp of the poem folding against
the power of the cat.
Possible use: to hold the bones of little ones
who cannot speak for themselves
or the Goddess Bastet.

Possible worth: treasure beyond speech
out of the old tomb, out of the mind's
sarcophagus. Wanting to touch
wanting to stare at her agate eyes
in the dark night of a museum postcard.

Bastet!
She moves toward me. She is here—
HISS HISS
With one paw raised
she scratches the final hieroglyphs
at the end of a bronze poem
I cannot see.

Because this was a command performance and did not arise from a moment of givenness or inspiration, the poem was a struggle. I worked on it
for three weeks, even taking it to Toronto with me where I visited the
ROM and found out that the sculpture was a sarcophagus probably in-
tended to hold the bones of a kitten. For some reason this information
was crucial in the development of the poem, and when I returned to
Edmonton I finished it in a state of total involvement and excitement. I
am not sure I like the poem very much, but I will not look a gift cat in
the whiskers. Though I will look a psychic in the eyes.

Eyes—all eyes—is that where we should look to discover the Creator Spirit? Or the Blessed Damozel leaning out a window of that old, old
house, laughing and crying, letting down the ladder of her hair.

SALT SPRING ISLAND, JULY 22-26, 1981

Imaginationɔ Companion

This isn't exactly a garland for Sharon Thesen. After all, she has Malcolm
Lowry, in *Confabulations*, saying, "I am murdered by the pistils / of mauve
orchids in a white vase." There's also a "Nosebleed like an opened tap /
pouring into my hands, tossed / like roses at the cheering crowd." Yet her
flowers, the subject of this little piece, she calls "imaginations companion, compadre / Without Blame." The lack of the possessive apostrophe
could possibly indicate that one cannot own or claim "*natura naturans*";
it also pluralizes "imagination" so that one is tempted to speculate on
the existence of different kinds of imaginations. For Thesen's flowers
operate in various ways in her wry lyricism. These virginal (until the
bees devour them), contingent beauties are there to be talked to, walked
with, observed, aesthetically enjoyed, caught in their dollar value, neighbour's pruning shears, their pain. For, yes, they seem to suffer, as the poet
does:

> . . . *The*
>
> painful yellow tulips
> open & open & open.
>> "Evocation," *Holding the Pose*

and

> . . . crocuses sprout purple
> into January sunlight,
> poor little things.
>> "Discourse," *Holding the Pose*

and

> . . . the burning rhododendrons:
> crimson, pink, white   flesh
>> "Before Choice," *Holding the Pose*

I don't know what *The Secret Life of Plants* did to Ruskin's pathetic fallacy, but Thesen's consciousness is entirely twentieth century, despite her defense of a vocabulary that includes words like "soul," "beauty," and "spirit." In "Postscript to Duncan McNaughton," where the idea of perfection the tulips convey is most accurately observed and precisely stated, the word "perfect," in one form or another, occurs three times in a twelve-line poem, the third climactic entry in a sensuous description of their seductive colouration: "—And the color, yellow creasing the edges / of that perfect blushy red." Gorgeous stuff, followed by the lyrical abstraction of:

> O *natura naturans*
> imaginations companion, compadre
> Without Blame
>
> "Postscript to Duncan McNaughton,"
> *Artemis Hates Romance*

Without Blame? I slant over to the *I Ching*; I open it at random—chance is chance, after all—to hexagram number sixty-two, "Preponderance of the small," in which the phrase "no blame" occurs twice in the interpretation of the lines. The commentary says that one is in position to correct one's mistakes in the right way. If we amend mistakes by a return to the right path, no blame remains. We are in the territory of Thesen's own moral imperatives. Her tulips are without blame not because they have mistakes to amend, but because we do; they are our guiding stars, emblematic of our own lost innocence, gone beauty, fallen grace, our cracked ideal forms.

The flowers appearing in her first three books, *Artemis Hates Romance*, *Holding the Pose*, and *Confabulations, Poems for Malcolm Lowry*, occur repeatedly, though not, I think, all that consciously, mainly in two ways: either besmirched by men, falsified and degraded, or as blooming talismans of perfection, goodness, love, aesthetic delight, and as symbols of the creative lyric impulse.

> The defoliated
> imagination is the end

of all lyric. The rose deformed
& the daisy impotent
& the poet dance
to no sound but
the sound stolen from God.
"Day Dream," Artemis Hates Romance

In our time "defoliation" has sinister overtones of Agent Orange, Vietnam, and the local highways department. Poetry and imaginations must struggle for survival. Each flowery appearance intensifies the sense of compadre, companion: *an associate, comrade; a person paid to live or travel with another; one of a pair or set.* The companion shares jeopardy and violence, springs up to ward off the Evil Eye, or just plain evil:

Picked up the photos of the land-
lord's dahlias, along the street
nothing but buses and sirens, dark
weather as I took a peek, saw spiky blossoms
ruby red and pale yellow
between faces and the dog. Not exactly

pictures of Treblinka, yet. . . .
"Nevado Del Ruiz," Malahat #77

Or their virginal innocence is defiled:

The gray-faced neighbour
clears his
phlegmy throat
before stooping
into the car,
spits
into the lilac bush.
"Ladies Advice," Malahat #72

That gratuitous insult is like a slap in the face or worse. Flowers are usually seen as female and sexual, and in women's poetry their presence might seem dangerously self-reflexive. There's an interesting absence of carnivorous blooms, e.g., the Venus fly trap, in the poetry of Sharon Thesen, though she comes close with those murderous "pistils of mauve orchids" that so scared Malcolm Lowry. Or their absence might reflect geographical exactitude—the west coast doesn't produce an abundance of floral carnivores, except in greenhouses where sexy orchids also grow. The female imagination prefers to image her companions as spontaneous perfect form and colour, unselfconscious, pure as the lilies of the field. Or she relates them to the airiness and movement of non-syntactic music:

> In this sweet and sour season
> Mozart and the incredible blossoms
> dance without a permit
> > "Season of No Bungling," *Holding the Pose*

But Thesen never promised us a rose garden, and in "Turquoise Carnations" she considers the intrusive mentation, warped aesthetics, and sick fancy that can skewer the talismanic ideal of "*natura naturans*":

> . . . Embarrassing turquoise carnations
> await a bad eye for beauty
> at the corner store, perhaps
> they dye them to hold something up
> against the news. Like bad poetry.
> > *Holding the Pose*

If, on the whole, her flowers are radiant bystanders to the events of news and history, they virtually disappear in a poem of personal displacement and alienation called "Radio New France Radio" (*Holding the Pose*). It's about her time in Montreal, that city where "the Saturday night cabs / honk & sidle up & down / the snowy streets." There is only one reference to flowers in its dozen pages close to the end when unnamed walkers are "bitten" by un-named blossoms "extravagant & common." A street clown's spastic act, beige hills, a dry cleaner in another language, displaced flamenco dancers, late night bad TV, a sky yellow and greasy are all depressed presences in the depressed atmosphere of the poem. Thesen's natural landscape seems to be the west coast where the preponderance of the small rectifying moments of being are enough in evidence through all four seasons to offer hope, hope that is nevertheless so minimal, perhaps illusory, it can only be caught in unguarded moments. The resulting lyricism is usually undercut and given that Thesenesque bitter, sardonic twist:

> Crimson gladiolus
> in a shop window
> nearly brings me to tears—
> call the poet
> a love poet
> then watch her hands—
> you'd be surprised
> what she does
> with the roses.

> "Lecture Noir," *Holding the Pose*

This undercutting is characteristic of Artemis who hates romance. Of course, Artemis *really* loves romance, or would love *a* romance, a corsage for the prom, etc., but she knows only too well that the phlegmy neighbour will probably spit in the lovely lilac face. Hence Thesen's valuing of "strife" in a poem. "By strife," she says in "A Few Notes on Poetry," "I mean the awareness, during the act of writing, of the field that we are in: the apparent 'tradition'; the forces of repression both inside and outside; the freshly-prepared ground of the contemporary (innovation, influence, pleasures, displeasures), and the tone of the culture generally—and these are just for starters." Her constant yet un-nervous awareness in her own poem-making allows this strife to keep the poem in motion, up in the air, falling on its face and getting up again. It's a dangerous and hard-won freedom she continually seeks, unbounded, broken through to, achieved, like the painful yellow tulips, by opening and opening and opening:

So stop crying. Get up. Go out. Leap
the mossy garden wall
the steel fence or whatever
the case may be & crash
through painted arcadias,
fragments of bliss & roses
decorating your fists.

"Praxis," Holding the Pose

In *Confabulations*, strife dominates the life of the poems, the mystery of redemption is left unsolved, the last lines of the last poem telling us "a mockingbird / pipes the morning in." And even in Wordsworth country the daffodils for Lowry are merely background to "oh bleak / bleak days of separation / from self & catastrophic states of mind." Thesen's use of a shifting "I"—first-person voice of Lowry and/or the poet (compassionate, one of a pair or set)—in this her most objective work, allows us to read that single, solitary line, italicized in the text, "*where I am it is dark,*" as either Lowry's condition or hers. Sharon Thesen did not choose her subject casually. Lowry, larger than life, is also one of her imaginations companions—not Without Blame but to whom one must attend, artist, writer ("you no wrider / you an espider"), *compadre*:

Alone in the garden
after a violent night
he kisses the bright pink faces
of peonies along the fence
tasting bees & the hereafter.

Confabulations

1988

Gabrielle Roy's Windflower

"So what is the news of the world?" Elsa Kumachuk asks her Uncle Ian when he returns from a trip across the river to the new Fort Chimo:

> He said it was foolish beyond belief. The same little soldiers they'd seen freezing here at the time of the second world war were perhaps getting themselves soaking wet on the other side of the world, in Korea where the United States had another squabble on its hands.

By the time the novel ends, the Vietnam War has also touched this little community in the vast emptiness of northern Quebec. Gabrielle Roy's global awareness informed much of her work, but with something more than just "the news of the world." She saw, or perhaps glimpsed, like a mirage on a distant horizon, a truly human race being born, if only out of the wreckage of conflict. But what fascinated her as a writer was the flawed and various human spectacle seen at close range.

Roy was in her fifties when she wrote *Windflower*, her experience and wisdom providing the narrator of the story with a kindly and some-times amused omniscience. This voice, soft as wind chimes, leaves us with the harmonics of sadness, our anger and outrage muted. Yet *Windflower* begins with a rape, includes incest, and probes the effects of white technology and culture on the Inuit. Who is this narrator who says, "In testimony then, here is the story, just as it is told in those parts, of Elsa, daughter of Archibald and Winnie Kumachuk"? Not an Inuit, surely—perhaps a pastor or priest, or an older white inhabitant (male? female?), for there's something condescending in that amused omnis-cience, guiltless, invisible.

Roy's last novel, though not her last book, *Windflower* is the second of her northern novels, the first being *The Hidden Mountain* in which she worked out her aesthetic philosophy of "*l'artiste solitaire et solidaire.*" *Windflower* first appeared in French as *La rivière sans repos* (1970) and included three short stories, or novellas, also dealing with technology's impact on the Inuit. Isolated, this slim volume has a poetic intensity, a formal and lyric beauty necessarily missing from a larger work like *The Hidden Mountain*. Closer to *The Road Past Altamont* and *Where Nests the Water Hen*, yet structurally and thematically more complex, *Windflower* is unique among Roy's fiction, as distant as Ungava or a new-born star from the urban realism of her densely populated first novel, *The Tin Flute*.

In this "tragic desert," this "petrified ocean" (the Inuit would see signs of life even in winter), the drama of "progress" for the Kumachuk family unfolds amid the shifting perspectives of far horizons and dingy huts, of vast sky and man-made windows, arctic sun and oil-lit lamps, the frozen sea without and "the frozen sea within" (Kafka's phrase). And always that clear-eyed narrator controlling how events appear to us, the pace of occurrences, the modest human scale of ambitions and hopes, distancing us somewhat from the awful pain of this tragedy of acculturation, ourselves invisible, guiltless, gliding along the liquid prose, fluid even in translation. And doesn't this slim volume *feel* light? Amazing.

Elsa, Jimmy, Thaddeus, Winnie, Archibald, Ian—the names! Obviously, the English missionaries got to Fort Chimo before the French to provide new identities, a new religion, and a new language for these ancient nomads who didn't know they were so deficient. The trajectory of their story forms a sort of loop out from the nexus of the two Fort Chimos, into the drifts and blizzards of the tundra where the turning point both literally and figuratively occurs—and back along the slopes of defeat to the New. This journey from new to old and back to the future pursues the question, how to live? Given the news of the world, not to mention the news from home, this question with all its existential implications is, I think, more important than the simpler one of how to survive.

How to live? Well, we can go to the movies ("two shows a week: one for the whites, one for the Eskimos"), as Elsa and her girlfriends (Lily, Mildred, Mary Jane) have just done when the novel opens. They giggle about this horribly ugly—and funny—man, Clark Gable. And Kissing! Hilarious, *disgusting*. This scene of youthful freshness and laughter (the laughter fades as the story progresses) introduces the important recurring image of the cinema and encapsulates at least two themes: the temptation and alienation of the Inuit by white culture, and the mystery and confusions of love. This scene on the fine and heavily symbolic straight road, American built, where we've seen the girls, arms linked, pigtails flying, leads directly to the rape of Elsa by the nameless G.I. She's left puzzled and pregnant but not terribly concerned (who *is* this narrator?), the act of rape echoing the larger intensities of economic and political violations. Even southern Canadians have occasionally appeared unconcerned at uninvited attentions until the bundle of joy turns out to be a mixed blessing.

And Jimmy is mixed, and a blessing for Elsa. Arriving in mock heroic fashion, like a little god, or a new star in their sky, he provides Elsa with a pretty good answer to the question, how to live? Become a mother. The theatricality of his appearances in the community, the performance of the bath ritual, the costuming of this treasured blue-eyed infant, the light that surrounds his little "golden topknot" bring his mother great joy at first and a gratifying sense of purpose. Critics sometimes refer to *Windflower* as a typical Roy story of devoted motherhood, but motherhood is always problematic in her work. Despite the charming scenes of natural harmony between mother and child, especially those by the river, something is wrong, for "her soul was so preoccupied with him it had no room for anyone else." Inspired by the example of her employer, Mme. Beaulieu (how to live *well*), propelled by her mania for buying, buying, for washing and cleaning, and doing things by the clock, disturbing the free easiness of her own family, Elsa enacts the craziness of the urban south in this desert of the north:

> Suddenly Elsa, whom no one had ever seen crying before, dissolved in tears. How odd it was to see her, once so gay, weeping, arms hanging at her sides, in the centre of the cabin.

Something is wrong—imitation, the inauthentic, seduction, loss of freedom, the cage.

The dramatic three-part structure of the novel allows for an abrupt scene shift to old Fort Chimo across the river Koksoak, site of dreams and decisions, and the emergence in Part II of the thinking, reading, teaching Elsa. Gone the high heels, gone Mme. Beaulieu's cast-off hats, the servant girl's black dress and little white crown, gone Mme. Beaulieu with her incomprehensible grief. Gone the alluring plate glass window of the H.B.C. Gone Thaddeus, Winnie, and Archibald. Enter Uncle Ian to show Elsa how to live, now, by way of the past.

This scruffy idyll of the simple life places extraordinary emphasis not only on the retrieval of the past, but on intellect and spirit, on written language: the fading inscriptions in the cemetery (cf. Roy's "Garden in the Wind"), Jimmy's lessons, Elsa's letter to Elizabeth Beaulieu, Ian's Bible, the reading of *Ivanhoe*, in short, on teaching, learning, and memory. Now interior and exterior spaces seem to merge; Jimmy is a calmer and happier child; something like domestic peace is achieved. As Elsa said when she found her grandmother's grave, "We came just in time." But no. Too late. "Perhaps she and her people had never become quite used to the presence among them of the police—a reminder of the endless increase of constraints."

When at the merest hint she might lose her son, Elsa fled with Jimmy to the old Fort, so now she and Ian take flight from the white policeman (nice M. Beaulieu) and his law that says Jimmy must go to school. There's something almost archetypal, or perhaps just cinematic, about this escape across the tundra by dog sled in a raging blizzard, with its sexual and emotional climax. The graphically described incestuous moment in the igloo is like the last act of a dying tribe when how to survive ousts how to live.

If the reader now turned to Mordecai Richler's opus *Solomon Gursky Was Here* (1989), the change in key from Gabrielle Roy's gentle register to Richler's raucous croak would come as something of a shock. In Richler, nothing is sacred, not even the iconic Gabrielle Roy, for among his parade of parodies one finds the flight into the arctic wastes replayed not just once, but twice, when Ephraim abducts his grandson, Solomon, and takes off with a yapping dog-team for the Polar Sea, and again when Solomon's brother and his "halfbreed" son head north in snowmobiles to administer the Jewish rites to the natives. There are nineteen years between the publication of the two books, and I think the change in sensibility is noteworthy. Richler seems immensely entertained by his garrulous characters (as we are), whereas Roy cohabits with hers in solidarity (as we do). There are no shamanic fireworks like Richler's in

Windflower, only the steady light of Thaddeus' wisdom. I suspect this "man of conciliation and peace," this half-blind artist in stone comes close to Gabrielle Roy's own moral centre and artistic code.

In contrast to Thaddeus, Ian's chronic anger, his self-defeating isolation, even his refusal to adapt to the white intruders undermine his knowledge and strength. Archibald as a character is droned out by the sound of his machines, Winnie stalled somewhere between the old and the new, sugaring and smoking her way to extinction. All these secondary characters, with their assigned schematic functions, fill out the portrait of an indigenous community in decline. Ian disappears, the others die, even Thaddeus, as if to manifest the death of the old ways, the defeat of a people.

A return to dream time for Elsa in Part III completes what has been called the pendulum movement of *Windflower*. Driven from one extreme to another for the sake of Jimmy, "child of mankind," she finally comes to rest in her old shack by the Koksoak, so like Winnie now, "the human being she was least anxious to resemble." Gone the years of cranking out souvenirs on her perpetual motion machine—a bitter counterpoint to Thaddeus' unhurried art—gone the spacious hut between the Anglican and Catholic missions, gone the consuming goods, bike, hockey gear, baseball bat, hamburger, gone pride, purpose, Jimmy. Even a pinball machine wouldn't have kept the morose teenager in Fort Chimo. Belonging nowhere, he takes to the air. His last words fall out of the sky like aromatic bombs.

Just as Elsa tried to turn rape into romance, so now, radio to ear, gazing into space, she transforms war into a fiction of love and regeneration, releasing the shy theme of the birth of a truly human race first uttered by old Inez in the cemetery. How to live.

We last see Elsa Kumachuk by the shores of her wild river, "a little more worn, a little more bowed," gathering a pebble here, a bird's egg there, "or some of those plant filaments, as delicate, soft and silky as the hair of a child, that are made to carry migratory seeds far into the distance." Windflower.

An Inuit telling this story would, of course, tell us another. And if some Elsa or Ian picked up this volume, would it feel so light? But I'm glad Roy risked imagining her Fort Chimoans. Mordecai Richler's pa-

rodic vision may be more in tune with his off-key times, but the expan-
sive sympathy of Gabrielle Roy, *l'artiste solitaire et solidaire*, transmits a
timeless and humane message retrieved from the news of the world.

1991

Unearned Numinosity

Names are numinous and never negligible
                                        Gavin Ewart

During a reading at the World Poetry Festival last spring in Toronto
(May 1986), I vowed I would stop using proper names in my poetry after
that reading; that I would deliver myself of the sin of unearned numinosity.
This was greeted with laughter and enthusiastic applause. My avowal of
poetic purity and self-improvement was obviously long overdue. Because
there were many poets in the audience that night, there was also the
pleasure of a vice shared, acknowledged, and understood.

Let the chipmunk praise the Lord as he bounds up Jacob's Ladder.
                      Anne Sexton, "O Ye Tongues"

In the course of that reading, my last chance, I flaunted such famous
personages as Winnie and Nelson Mandela, Cory Aquino, Henry Miller,
Picasso, Ezra Pound, Ghalib, Paul Horn, William Yeats, bill bissett, John
Thompson, Rodin, Parsifal, Einstein and Bohr. And Phyllis. I'd been
aware of this naming habit for some time, but the urge to name was
insistent, and just as I keep on smoking I even now continue to name.

Names are charged, are numinous partly because the sounds they
produce are not always to be found in common nouns—and are seductive, provocative, proper, and odd: Ezra, Vasarely, Edith, Rilke,
Nebuchadnezzar. Also, names import into poems, (f.o.b.) a culture clus-
ter of politics, history, philosophy, art, literature, in short, an ethos. In
the economy of the poem this poetic shorthand records faces, bodies,
gestures, styles of action.

Let Ishmael dedicate a Tyger, and give praise for the liberty in which
The Lord has let him at large.
                              Christopher Smart, *Jubilate Agno*

Let Anne and Christopher appear with two robins whose
worms are sweet and pink as lipstick.
                          Anne Sexton, "O Ye Tongues"

Because names are normally capitalized they stand out in the text, behaving as stressed notes, visually and aurally:

I'll read Keats and eye the weather too,
smoke cigarettes, watch Captain Kangaroo.
                          John Thompson, *Stilt Jack*

Pace bill bissett and e.e. cummings.
     Names introduce individuals as incipient characters in a possible
story, liberating energy in the poem, a dramatic note in the poet's register—a theatrical voice, a stamp of the foot:

Yeats. Yeats. Yeats. Yeats. Yeats. Yeats. Yeats.
Why wouldn't the man shut up?
                          John Thompson, *Stilt Jack*

Or the anti-lyrical impulse may emerge less dramatically as a slightly
hesitating waltz—Ah, Ghalib (pause)—a tête à tête, or a conspiratorial
séance:

For I pray that Kayo who smiles from the photo above me
from his lawn chair in Bermuda will smile at his name among tongues.
                          Anne Sexton, "O Ye Tongues"

If the poem is a narrative, epic, ballad, dramatic monologue, or stories in verse like *The Canterbury Tales*, characters have a chance to develop lives of their own. But in the kind of scatter effect I and many
other modern poets use, the free-fall may sound like name-dropping where
the payoff can be heard as an accretion of power, prestige, or guilt by
association. Despite Julia's clothes and Wordsworth's Milton, I still feel
slightly guilty for the liberties I take with others' fame, glory, and excel-
lence. Many poets, though, indulge themselves in dedicating poem after

poem to well-known or unknown individuals (beloved, hated, admired, dismissed, mocked, imitated), a more studied method of practising the magic of the never negligible and numinous naming. My bow to an individual usually takes place within the poem itself.

Jung claimed that the obsessive or possessive force, or energy, discharged in an encounter with an archetypal figure *is* numinosity. *Numinous* means the combined feeling of attraction and awe—our sense of communion with divinity. Mere mortals can be magical too; when we utter or mutter a name we are in the allure of the numinous. The charismatic ones, living or dead, shine forth in our speaking and together we say, "I am":

> *For birth was a disease and Christopher and I invented the cure.*
> *For we swallow magic and we deliver Anne.*
> Anne Sexton, "O Ye Tongues"

The naming instinct, like the homing instinct, seems to come with the territory. The manna should not be resisted and what a stupid vow I took. Great poets live with divine spirits; the rest of us with familiar, with household gods, who, if you cry, may hear you:

> *For I will consider my Cat Jeoffry. . . .*
> *For he can tread to all the measures upon the musick.*
> Christopher Smart, *Jubilate Agno*

1987

The Crannies of Matter: Texture in Robin Blaser's Later "Image-Nations"

When I was writing my review of Robin Blaser's collected poems, *The Holy Forest* (1993), for *Books in Canada*, I knew I wanted to return at a later date to a statement I made then: "From the relative simplicity of 'Image-Nation 1,' about a cat giving birth, and perhaps the birth of language, to the increasing technical and intellectual complexity and dense textures of the final ones, we attend the development of a major artist." The date I wanted to keep was with those "dense textures."

I thought I knew what I meant, if only vaguely, by our use of the word texture as we apply it to poetry, but the later "Image-Nations" from, say, numbers twenty-two to twenty-five, seemed to require a more rigorous exploration of that somewhat worn-out metaphor, almost an abstraction now, so distant from its source.

I used to think of texture in poetry as mainly a sound apparition produced by an intricate play of vocables whose plosives, dentals, labials, fricatives, hoots, whistles, yells and chuckles, sighs, murmurs, phonemic and syllabic interactions could scuff up or smooth out the surface of a poem. Cacophony, sonority, plainsong created by the way consonants keep company with riverine vowels—assonance, consonance, alliteration and their often mimetic effects—are also part of the microstructure. Linguistic intensifications through the use of other languages and alphabets, quotations, dialogue, prose passages, and so on, affect textural values. And, of course, *vocabulary* swanning around managing a variety of rhythmic manoeuvres (mating with syntax) is major mover.

The mix of metaphors in that paragraph is not entirely accidental. When we speak of texture in poetry we're in the land of mixed metaphors, or, more accurately, in the surreal world of synesthesia where sensory perceptions seem to be cross-wired and the sky today is a high C, or the high C sounds like cerulean blue. For texture primarily refers to something we can touch, like the threads of a fabric. We put out our hand and feel it, rub it against the face, experience its silkiness or tweedy burr, even with our eyes closed. Eyes opened, we also see its design effect. But run your hand over a page of poetry and all you feel is the paper's texture—a simplistic observation, simply pointing to the importance of the visual aspect of poetic texture. The way the poem is deployed on the plane of the page, its notation and aesthetic interest, is what strikes the reader first: the type used, colour of ink, ratio of black or blue or brown or red to white or grey or ivory; stanzaic pattern, shape of the poetic field, a thickening here of multisyllabic words, a traffic jam of X's, K's, Z's, G's, a thinning there of the micromass in monosyllables, a stream of vowels; the dribble of type in a concrete outburst, decorative typographical devices, as well as pictograms, hieroglyphs, drawings. Punctuation! The whole shebang of the two-dimensional design surface pulls the reader into the poem, invites, challenges or repels us. Robin Blaser's "Image-Nation 1" looks lighter, more conventional with its obvious stanzaic pattern and its aligned left-hand margin than "Image-Nation 25," which appears denser, more complicated, difficult, irregular, tantalizing.

When we *sound* a poem aloud the synesthesic transfer that takes place to give us a sense of texture occurs because—simplicity itself—words are formed inside the chest and head, inside the mouth. Just as tofu feels different in texture from peach fuzz, so a word like "synecdoche" feels different in the mouth from "sibylline" or "pataphysical" as it knocks against the sound-box, struggles over and under the tongue, hits the palate, rolls around in saliva, scrubs the teeth, hissing and croaking its way out through lips, guided by ears, propelled, expelled by the breath. *In your face. Holes of intelligence. The crannies of matter.*

But the poem which the eyes see is outside ourselves, an artifact. The sense of touch turned on by the eyes (even without the help of an optical third dimension) is charged by the poem's thingness, its design and structure. Indeed, one of the definitions of texture is structure and is, the dictionary tells us, "the mode of union or disposition of elementary constituent parts . . . ; minute structure or make; structural order. . . ." (Funk & Wagnalls). If we were reading the poem in Braille we'd have a bird in the hand.

This exploratory surgery separating sound and sight, the poem heard and the poem read, serves to allay anxiety and keep the lab in business. The function of texture, visual and aural, is to give pleasure, create interest, and involve the reader or listener in the poem's meaning and affect. There's no easy way (for me) to talk about it: boundaries will over-lap, metaphors will mix, content and form can't be separated, and meaning, with its fluctuating auras, will interfere with single-mindedness:

<pre>
                      the Event
          was an activity turned in
          all directions
                      of what contained them,
          and retraced
                      the wing of the world showed,
              who is companion • blue-hued • well-marked
                      "Image-Nation 11 (the poesis" (136-7)
</pre>

To begin at the beginning, for comparison's sake and to gather our wits, we should look at, listen to Robin Blaser's first offering in the "Image-Nations," his long, perhaps unending, serial poem. In attempting to define this genre, Blaser wrote: "The poems tend to act as a sequence of energies which run out when so much of a tale is told. I like to describe this in Ovidian terms, as a *carmen perpetuum*, a continuous song in which the fragmented subject matter is only apparently disconnected" (Foreword, xiv). That's not the whole story, but now the poem:

<pre>
          Image-Nation 1 (the fold
          the participation is broken
          fished from a sky of fire
          the fiery lake pouring itself
          to reach here

          that matter of language caught
          in the fact so that we
          meet in paradise in such
          times, the I consumes itself
</pre>

white trees, rings around them,
wander and roll, the fog breaks,
the sky, blue in the window

sits up there, out of reach
hand full of *beautifuls-uglies,*
justs-unjusts, halves-doubles,
pulls the strings, I saw the cat

the births begin on the bed,
shaped as it is
by a god, four kittens
when they are there
she comes to his feet

picked up and held, she
fills his hand with blood
the red pool flows over
his silver ring, drips
to the floor

the language sticks to
his honey-breath she is
the path of a tale, a door
to the perishing moonshine,
holes of intelligence
supposed to be in the heart

(61)

Now look at, listen to these lines from "Image-Nation 25 (Exody,":

when Proto-Indo-European trees walked in Eden—delight in life—
at the edge of the glaciers, the apple among them, *requiring mini-*
mum cold for its winter dormance—trying to say, in *primitive semantics,*
my love *abvl- and *mahlo—north and south—walking among them
west, some small thing, man or woman, *universal and unconfined in*

its relations—hewing down a tree with a stone axe, the physical difference
between an elm and a linden, or even an English and a live oak, would be
obvious—calluses—gone to thought—apple-cheeks, my love

(368)

The differences in appearance, sound, and technique are striking, and why shouldn't they be when thirty years stretch between the two compositions? The first "Image-Nation" is easily musical and still attached to the lyric mode; the later one looks like prose (an illusion) and is full of linguistic lore, rhythmic variables, textural density, the data grid crammed with "that matter of language caught / in the fact." Notionally, what attracted me to place these passages one below the other was the persistence of those restless trees—wandering and rolling around like toddlers in foggy Paradise in number 1, evolved and *walking*, perhaps just to keep warm, in cold Eden in number 25. These trees are poetic relatives of those catalogued at epic length in Ovid's very long but un-epic poem *Metamorphoses* (Book X, 227), the ones that crowd around Orpheus, moved to move closer by his gorgeous music.

Because of the Ovidian influence on the "Image-Nations" we can reasonably expect to be lured by musical tale-telling and the presence of transformational events. Other themes and intentions expressed in "Image-Nation 1" are "that matter of language caught / in the fact," i.e., a devotion to the concrete, the real; the ways and means by which the "*holes of intelligence*" create the body of knowledge and art—love's body; the birth of language; Paradise lost, regained and lost again; the ways "the I consumes itself." And the fold. The fold is a persistently recurring icon in Blaser's work, carrying an almost hermetic or religious intensity, representing the *mysterium*, the secret numinous thing at the heart of the matter, the "unfolded fold."

(Perhaps "themes" is not the right word to describe the process at work in the serial poem. Ideas, images, texts, friends, scenes are discovered and re-discovered as if by chance, by synchronicity and aleatoric correspondences. These arrive from "outside" as givens, received like dictation and copied down by the poet.)

• ◡

I have a vision of Robin Blaser's study, which I've never entered, except via letters. He's at his desk in the morning, dressed in a long forest-green bathrobe, "ungroomed," tousled white hair metallic and awry, coffee, the third one, being consumed. His letters have disclosed this much of the vision. The books that line the walls don't just stand there in ranks, well-behaved. No, they're wandering around like his Edenic trees, lolling, sprawling, gazing enviously out at the free-floater birds in the ancestral tree. And then one, two, three alight on his desk, flash themselves open at just the right page, *illuminated*, in front of the scholar-poet. They are his great and intimate companions whose presences he invites into the work—for a chat, an argument, a colloquy, an honoured place in the lines. As they land in their new habitat they tend to alter the surface tensions of the poem, setting up new vibrations and visual effects. To use words like quotation or citation for these *illuminati* doesn't seem quite right. A mutual exchange seems to take place of gifts, of energies, of light—straight from the Holy Forest:

> *God, self, history, and book are,* Mark C. Taylor tells us, *bound in an intricate relationship in which each mirrors the other—*
> "Image-Nation 25 (Exody,"
> (367)

·◞

Notes, Impressions, Guidelines, and Data Clusters

Image-Nation 22 (in memoriam

This elegy on the death of Robert Graves is not, surprisingly, for Robert Graves the poet but Robert Graves the scholar/anthropologist/mythographer/de-mythographer. Author of *The White Goddess, The Greek Myths, The New Crete, The Nazarene Gospel Restored* (with Joshua Podro), *King Jesus,* and numerous other works.

The poem, I *think*, shows how Gravesian texts come to mind—Blaser's—at the news of the author's death, interconnected along an associational path, leading him to explore the archetypal duality suggested by the figure of the Goddess (in her multiple manifestations) as she is flared against the gods, the Patriarchs, and Jesus Christ. The poet attempts to make some human and historical sense of it all.

• ⟋

The terrain, verbal and material:
    The sacred groves and mountains of mythology and rock cliffs and rough roads of the Bible.

Little procedures for inducing textural variety:
    The use of *proper names* (embodying language) to people the actual and verbal landscape, creating OLWEN BLODEUWEDD *CIRCE* LAMIA RHIANNON *EZEKIEL* JEHOVAH *ZEUS* ENOCH NABU *THOTH HERMES* MOT ALEXANDER *AGGRATH BAT MACHLAT* SON OF MAN et al.;
    Italics for book titles, citations (gifts), intensity, *design elegance* in this ancient rough and tumble;
    Dashes—in Dickinsonian profusion—*East of Eden*—for fragmentary free associations, arrivals, interruptions, breath, a turn in all directions—retracings.

Major procedure for expressing thought and varying surface tensions:
    Prose-like paragraphs with variable right margins, loosely containing all of the above and arranging Blaser's argument re the patriarchal bias of received history and its language.

Mood, Measure, Tone:
    A sense of *loss* running under the *slow movement* of the composition. But Blaser isn't raising a monument to Robert Graves; he is too involved with the work, with sorting things out, his argument in this somewhat anti-elegiac elegy. Though the poem is massive in its implications and in the way it is "built," the a-phasic alternation of prosaic passages with poetic ones—and the amazing sonic range and rhythmic invention this method allows—deflects any tendency towards epic grandeur and the heroic. Or, if heroic, then only if we interpret the scholar's life-work, his mental excavations of the middens of the deep past, as heroic, as well we might.

Layers, folds, reflecting surfaces, flaking parchment, moonscapes:

> their squeezed were there and breasts their handled were
> /Oholah (were) names their And .nipples virgin
> Mine were they And .sister her, Oholibah and oldest the
> /sons bore they

and

> and Oholah (is) Samaria :names their And .daughters and
> /whored And .Oholibah (is)Jerusalem
> . . . Me under Oholah
> (*Ezekiel* 23:4-6)
> (322)

Read this passage from left to right and it sounds like a Language or a sound poem, but go from right to left, as instructed in the line immediately below this bright poem within the poem, and the scroll unfolds, or the tablet faintly shows a sane syntax, flaked. This disruption in the onward movement of our reading is total as one stops to puzzle it out and marvel at the diversion. The truth is laughter. *Oholah. Oholibah.* (Samaria. Jerusalem.)

•◞

And then there are the LISTS or CATALOGUES of NOUNS, in this poem, from Ezekiel's chariot of fire:

> *Amber*
> *Fire-Garnet ('the terrible crystal')*
> *and Sapphire*
>
> (321)

Minute poetic seizures. Polished gems. Reflecting surfaces. And more, from the biblical world:

> gods   terebinth
>   thunder
>   pomegranate

                    bull
                    goat
                    antelope
                    calf

                    . . .

                                        (322)

                            ·و

                    ISHTAR
resonates in her central position on the poem's third and last page
We cannot avoid her
                    sun and starlight, wife of Tammuz, goddess of
                    LOVE & FESTIVITY
Even among *the ruins of the real*
                            & WAR

                            ·و

From "Image-Nation 4 (old gold"
                    . . .

                    this is a surface of the moon
                    black and crusted . . .

                    . . .   if you walk
                    unwary, your feet slip into the
                    fire of strawberries . . .
                                        (64)

We can read these lines as a guide to Blaser's poetic procedures, his prin-
ciple of *randonnée* or receptivity, and as directions for our own readerly
response, as
    if all the heavens were parchment, and all the trees pens, and
    all the seas ink, . . .

                                        (323)

Magical, sad, witty inversions and transformations. *As if.* If we happen to fall through to the little poem hidden beneath this sigh—

> If all the Earthe were paper white
> and all the seas were incke
> Twere not enough for me to write
> as my poore hart do^th thinke.
>
> (John Lyly, 1554?-1666)

—then the elegy ends on exactly the right note **in memoriam** with its Tennysonian sob and dying fall. But if we stay on top with the argument, then the lines might be read as a critique of man-the-manufacturer, exploiter of nature. The scholarly life might also be seen as unnatural, unspontaneous.

•⤸

Postscript. A letter arrives (2/21/95) from Robin answering a question I'd asked him about the provenance of the italicized lines, "*as if all the heavens . . .*" As well as Lyly "tucked away in [his] heart," he explains that "these lines are quotation—they are rabbinical—Podro led me to them—but I can't find, at the moment, the name of the Rabbi." It's the quarrel between the Hebraic and the Platonic traditions that interests him. He also says that number 22 was first written to celebrate Graves's eightieth birthday, then re-worked later. Erasure—or strawberry fields forever?

> and Brancusi thought of it, surfaces which are depths
> brought to light and shadow, Eve and Plato flickering
> side by side. . . .
>
> "Image-Nation 23 (imago mundi" (328-9)

•⤸

Image-Nation 23 (imago mundi

This is a poem about SCULPTURE. The books are taking a nap. This is a poem about *abstraction* and *public art*. "Man's" fate as a TILTED RED CUBE (by Noguchi), the bronze hero knocked off his big bronze horse. A fall out of ethnocentricity into civility, right proportion, A WORLD VIEW.

‿

Terrain:

All-weather public space: *agora,* plaza, courtyard, square, park, public garden.

Pitch:

Mi-voix, level-headed, perfect.

‿

SCULPTURE / TEXTURE / TEXTUAL / CONTEXTUAL *in the public eye*

THE RHETORIC OF GRAND GESTURES *elided* into Brancusi's

Table of Silence   his   Gate of the Kiss
Noguchi's "Black Sun" in Seattle
"white marble garden at Yale"
OR THE RHETORIC dis-assembled in-to-
Du-champ's

HORSE LAUGH

at retinal folly, as he rummages through the kitsch of the cultural kitchen, his presence in the poem making room for *Robinesque* "dear mundane images" and another (dear) list of touchables—sex cylinder, desire-mag-neto, scissors, sieves, oculist witnessess, chocolate grinder, etc. Duchamp ("of the field") an unlikely collaborator with like-minded rhyming Noguchi/Brancusi. What they all three share is their project to de-cen-tre US into:

> . . . *a greater chaos*
> *and a new equilibrium art is an element in asymmetrical*
> *flux   no isolated object*
> *all function, all linkage*
> to our birthplace and back again

(330)

‿

"the unthought truth of materials," here, words on paper, available if

form opens   *space opens*

and a fresh breeze blows in

and   over

surfaces which are depths / brought to light and shadow

•‿

(*en français, enfin*:

sur-face,

over and under the form . . .

(329)

•‿

The talk, the philosophizing here is more relaxed, casual, though learned, verbally peripatetic—isn't it?—than the intellectual passion, the *deep song* of number 22. I am becoming almost languid just listening in on number 23, despite the Midway kick-start of Duchamp's "Large Glass" and the sculptural masses placed along the way. I'm gliding along on the semi-gloss of this silver room of a poem, its streamed lines so unobtrusive. . . . No argument, no contestation here, the poet happy in this good company, alone, afloat in his craft on Ink Lake, making a poem about Public Art, in abstraction, in *imag-i-nation*, a "Civil Elegy" sent aloft on a wing and a prayer, a paper crane.

•‿

You! Run your own tongue over the image nation, tell me about texture in the ear. And in "the eros of chances among things" as I turn to ask

this question: Why is British Barbara Hepworth
excluded from this scene?
Her Public Art
Her Scuplture Garden
"holes of intelligence"

66

For Goodness' Sake?

"Eve and Plato flickering / side by side" in the St. Ives rain and sun, in New York (too monumental, heroic?) at the *United Nations*—

abstraction is distance

(invisible the crannies of matter, burning and hidden,
burnished and folded in to the silent *sur-face* where
the I consumes itself

in praise

•و

Image-Nation 24 ('oh, pshaw,'

> *hwa has become 'what'*
> *hwa has also become 'who'*
> *hwan has become 'when'*
> *hwaer has become 'where'*
> "Image-Nation 10 (marriage clothes"

(133)

•و

WHAT: fragmented memoir of family life and beyond; familial history as social and linguistic history; anecdotal (narrative) prose poem.

WHO: the Folks—great-grandmother Ina, grandaunt Tina, grandmother Sophia (Dot, for short—the wise telegrapher), mother Ina Mae, father "Bob," the outsider, aunts, uncles, more grandparents, brother Gus, sister Hope, Robin, named for " 'an intruder and a calamity, of course.' "
<u>Glimpsed in passing</u>: Brigham Young, Benjamin West, Harriet Beecher Stowe, Emerson, Kublai Khan, Alfred North Whitehead, Italo Calvino, Michel de Certeau, George Bush, Pat Robertson, Pat Buchanan et. al. And " 'you,' my love."

WHEN: from distant Indo-European language past to Amer-Electronic present. Robin born/re-born in Denver, Colorado, 1925.

WHERE: Orchard, Idaho, in and around a railroad boxcar (yellow) converted into a house, having been derailed from its nearby tracks which follow the Portneuf River in all directions.

METHOD: babbling brook, stream of semi-consciousness, controlled torrent of rage, still waters, in that order.

EMBLEMS: Paradise Orchard (the family tree); yellow boxcar; the Golden Bible; rocking chair; library table.

CLIMATE: Spring-feverish; warm and sunny; in cold Hell.

·⤳

The coltish playfulness and verbal high-jinks presented on the first page of this very long "Image-Nation" remind me of the opening page of James Joyce's novel *A Portrait of the Artist as a Young Man*. Although Blaser doesn't regress to actual baby-talk like Joyce's baby Stephen, he does indulge in some self-amused infantile word-play, gurgling and gargling *g* sounds with gusto: God, gawdelpus, gawking, giddy, bigots, by-gods, godbwyes, gossips, godsibbs—"kin of some Indo-European past participle—*ghat . . . an epithet of Indra—Mind." Oh pshaw! Drat! Have you got a toy-box? That question asked in an earlier poem called "writing table" is here answered again as the cheeky Robin junior and Robin senior wind up their talking toys just outside the boxcar ("mouthing back through the window") at the (great-grand) mother tongue:

> g & d retained become *gad, gawd, gud*
> or only the g becoming *gog, golly, gosh, gum*
> or disguise g as c and *cock, cor, cod* appear . . .
> (353)

A babbling brook of textures: begad, begar, bedad, egad, swounds, zounds . . . expletives touching and avoiding GOD whose Golden Bible will be encountered later in the poem in iconic form—"*the thin gold plates,*

eight inches square"—and in the debased versions of thundering Funda-
mentalism. From play, to prayer, to platitude.

> a neighbour in flowery pink gingham, puffed sleeves . . . leaned
> out of the sun, over the picket fence, and said, 'My,' leaving the
> expletive word God out, 'he has a big vocabulary'—
>
> (359)

• ⤴

Turn the page. Mr. Blaser, growing old, is in his armchair reminiscing
along the stream of semi-consciousness in tell-tale prose. *Simulated* prose,
prose *poem*. Full of anecdotes and characters, domestic scenes, epiphanies, songs, life passages, "jade moments," this "Image-Nation" gives us
story and history in a seemingly effortless way. Long prose poems do
tend toward narrative, "counterpoints of monads becoming nomads."
But can this sort of writing still be called "continuous song"? If so, what
kind of song? Well, what kind of songs are there? Art songs (German
Lieder), airs-arias, operatic recitative, blues, folk ballad, anthem, canti-
cle, threnody are some of the categories from which we might choose. A
New Dictionary of Music defines *ballad* as "old song (often a Folk Song)
telling a story . . . a self-contained song of a narrative nature. . . . " (Jacobs,
30). *Recitative* is defined as a "type of speech-like singing which is written in ordinary notation but in which a certain freedom of rhythm (and
sometimes in pitch) is allowed in performance" (311). Each definition is
helpful in maintaining, if too literally, Blaser's trope of *carmen perpetuum*,
encouraging us to hear the musical pattern so skillfully composed in this
poem of here today, gone tomorrow, "fold according to fold."

> now, the players tumble like spiky weeds—over Craters of the
> Moon—they collapse into their own Will—stretch out in tech-
> nology—do not recognize themselves—forgive themselves, un-
> aware and repetitious—the 'I' cannot exist there—it was
> glass in *an impossible body*—my lyric voice loose in it—
> tattoos of an absolute language—old song—
>
> (362)

As we say, "the story *unfolds*," or it's only "a *tissue* of lies," or a tale is *spun* or *woven* into a whole cloth of inter-connections, the weaver designing the outcome, the coming-out. Home-spun, moving out alone, or with " 'you,' my love," as in the broken song of the final lines of number 24 when "the ashen boy—becomes—exodic." Alien. Exotic.

·↵

Image-Nation 25 (Exody,

—the soul becomes a fracture in the old paint—like the surface of a moonlit Ryder painting—running joyous and jagged— here and there—

"Mappa Mundi" (365-6)

holes of intelligence
supposed to be in the heart
"Image-Nation 1 (the fold" (61)

the pleats of matter, and the folds of the soul
"Image-Nation 25 (Exody," (370)

·↵

Guiding lights:
crystal, glass, lenses, mirrors—refracting, reflecting, transparent, distorting.

View-finder:
up: cosmos; *down:* labyrinth; *straight ahead:* horizon.

Form:
"Sculptured thought."

Nothing distinguishes me ontologically from a crystal, a plant, an ani mal, or the order of the world; we are drifting together toward the noise and black depths of the universe . . . Michel Serres tells us. . . .

(367)

This *is* intertextuality where we are a very small part of the intertext in the planetary and inter-planetary ecology; we are suspended now in "*a greater chaos / and a new equilibrium.*" Relativity, probability, chance—we are their subjects, and they are ours:

> tourbillions, that is, whirlwinds, whirlpools, vortexes, fireworks, the writer writing twists there—his or her *chance-possessed breath*—
> (367)

Like a scene from Dante. As if to balance the hellish rapture of writing, we're given a mildly comic, domestic version of our poet, perhaps the story-teller of number 24, as a huge chest of drawers crammed with memories of "God, self, history, and book," the stuff of imagination.

It might be helpful in understanding this densest of the "Image-Nations" if we consider it as illustrative of the serial poem itself. According to the poet Jack Spicer, Blaser once described the arrival of a serial poem as something like this: "It's as if you go into a room, a dark room, the light is turned on for a minute, then it's turned off again, and then you go into a different room where a light is turned on and turned off" (*Poetics of the New American Poetry*, 233). Although this sounds as if something other than the poet is in charge of the poems, the poet is, finally, responsible for the actual made poem. We can see just how responsible in number 25 in the complex organization of its "Sculptured thought," and in its tri-partite structure which mirrors the triptych construction of Hieronymus Bosch's *The Garden of Earthly Delight*, the brilliant focal point of this poem.

This is a very large house. The light goes on and off several times in the library to reveal the books of Michel Serres, Mark C. Taylor, Paul Friedrich (the trees), Michel de Certeau, and Gilles Deleuze. These authors provide Blaser with some of his "wisdom books," and the brief passages used in number 25 are like meditation beads, providing the conceptual basis for the poem's procedures, its vast space-time scale, its grandeur: from cosmos to microcosmos, from Pleistocene to the present.

As I near the end of my tour of the later "Image-Nations," I see that concepts also contribute to texture, along with the aural and visual aspects discussed earlier. The poem heard, the poem seen, the poem thought. A sense of volume and mass generated by the concepts adds to the poem's thingness, creating surfaces "over and under the form." The operation producing this illusion has, perhaps, more to do with kinesthesia this time than synesthesia.

·~

A light is switched on in the great Hall of Mirrors where all is *"lapsus, disproportion, and inversion,"* a sort of metaphysical fun-house. Here the great triptych of Bosch is on display, that weird Paradise which Blaser, or, if you prefer, the persona, has been studying for forty years. He's brought along Michel de Certeau as his Virgil, his guide on entering the labyrinth of the painting. The light stays on long enough for him to pull out his magnifying glass to get a better look at the multiples in action. Once again, he engages the economy and precision of the list, or catalogue, in an attempt to render into language (reproducing a reproduction) the circles and ellipses, the inter-penetrating objects and bodies of the heavily populated scenes before him. This adherence to the concrete details of the painting (nothing but brush strokes) creates a language valley of burgeoning sounds and sights:

                              —a youth, bent backward,
            riding a spotted, kerchiefed cat, whose balls shine, highlighted—
            arrows, flowers, sticks, bird beaks stuck up asses—two figures
            shut up in a mollusc shell, one of them shitting a pearl—another

whose face looks back over his body and at us, a broken
egg shell with a tavern in it. . . .

(369)

"[A]n anal and oral poetics," according to de Certeau, who is quoted below the near epic-length list, "a marvelous animality of asses and mouths, a greedy flowering of amorous play—" (369).

Emerging from this labyrinth of colourful multiples folding in upon themselves, we are returned to the library where a text of Deleuze concerning the fold-like nature of the labyrinth is highlighted:

The multiple is not only what has many parts but what is folded in many ways. . . . A 'cryptographer' is needed, someone who can at once account for nature and decipher the soul, who can peer into the crannies of matter and read the soul.

(370)

A cryptographer is not provided for the reader climbing out of this labyrinth, but we are released into the resolved mind of the poet, lit up now with warm memories of the boxcar home, "the brilliance of reading under the library table," and the dismantled rocking chair with its painted back-rest. The poem ends serenely with a cantabile lift:

nevertheless, I rock there,
wandering Jew and nomad

I imagine mortality,
its unrest and proses

I imagine evolutionary love,

my thousand and one celebrations

(371)

The textures of a life well lived, of work well done, of gratified desire. The light goes off on the image nation. Until it goes on again.

1995

73

The Mind's Eye

A Photo-Collage Essay

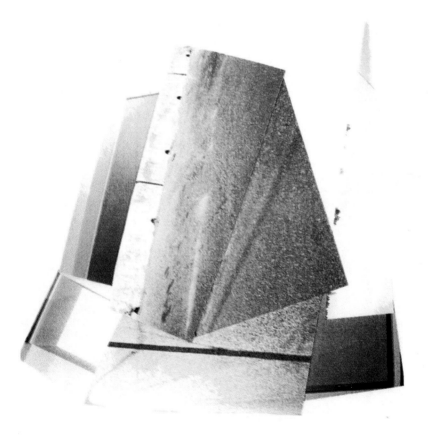

Tibetan Desire IV, *1993, 8 1/2″ x 11″*

Observatorium II, 1994, 11" x 17"

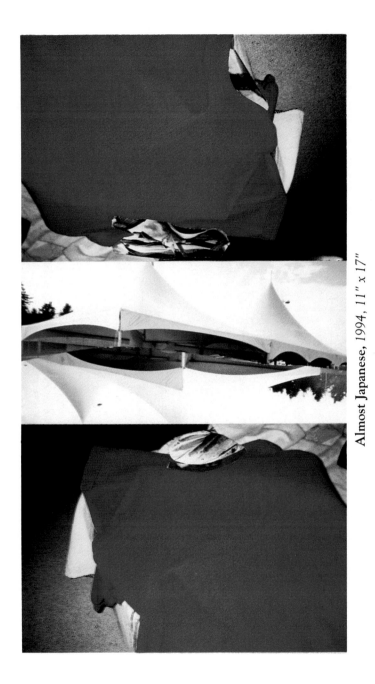

Almost Japanese, 1994, 11" x 17"

The Greek One, 1993, 8 1/2" x 11"

Night Space, 1994, 8 1/2" x 11"

Composition, *1995, 8 1/2" x 11"*

Wilson's Bowl IV, *1993, 8 1/2" x 11"*

Greg Curnoe Cycle IV, 1994, 8 1/2" x 11"

Might-have-been: The Tedious Shores

I might have been the first woman prime minister of Canada—that was the prediction in the year book when I graduated from U.B.C. I was very political then. In the amused and silly tone of year books, the mystery writers added that I'd hang chintz curtains in the House of Commons. It *was* 1949. Indeed, immediately after graduation I ran as a candidate in a provincial election, but knowing I'd lose. I was full of youthful idealism then, not political ambition.

A year or so later I moved to Montreal and had not a mystical experience but something like it which revealed to me that my destiny was to be a poet. This vocation was at least closer to the truth of me than the promise of the degenerative disease that is the life of a politician. In and around a variety of jobs and personae through the years I remained committed to being a poet. But now, though it hurts, I can sometimes be heard using the past tense, saying with a certain wryness, "I was a poet."

In the spring of 1993 I bought a new camera, an inexpensive, fully automatic Minolta Riva 35, and began to see in a subtly different way. Or had I begun to see in a different way and then bought the camera? I rushed around taking photographs, getting excited about my new view of things. At this time I also saw paintings, wild sprays of colour in my head, fantastic patterns. Do I have a brain tumour or should I take up painting?

I mentioned all this to my friend Sally Hulcoop, who then gave me a belated birthday present on July 4: watercolour paints, brushes, paper. An inspired gift. I tested out the colours on tiny sheets of a note-pad, doodles really, but the "ideas" came with ease. I moved on to the nicely textured paper of Sally's gift. I couldn't draw—never could—but some compulsion took over and I painted for three days. And stopped.

One night later in July, after midnight, I got out of bed like a sleep-walker, steered myself to some photographs, and began to cut them up.

At the kitchen counter I made my first collage. Where did this impulse come from? I don't know.

I do know I'd become short-sighted in the last couple of years, as often happens when cataracts are forming (this degenerative disease our lives). I like the symbolic significance of the long view, so often desperate, being eclipsed by the phenomenal close-up.

And now I was juggling the two activities: obsessively teaching myself how to paint, reading instructional art books, experimenting with tools, papers, paint, textures, techniques. For the quieter more meditative times, and with a certain mind-set, I sat in a chair with a tray by my side cutting up bits of photos, fussing with a composition until something clicked, like a jig-saw puzzle.

In the middle of August you might find me up at three in the morning trying out a new tube of violet or purple lake, attempting to capture the comet showers of the night sky. I'd probably been painting all day too, though painting is too fine a word to apply to an activity I'd never tried before; but I was learning. As the months passed so did my almost chronic depression. Painting my Prozac. Collages my keeper. Colour my chemical. I was possessed. Then the alarming questions arose: should I have been an artist? Have I been on the wrong course most of my life? Did I skip an incarnation? A gut-wrenching, if momentary, realization:

> My name is Might-have-been;
> I am also called No-more, Too-late, Farewell.

How convenient to find Dante Gabriel Rossetti's words at hand, Rossetti the poet-painter described in *The Reader's Encyclopedia* as a painter who "had little formal training, revealed little technical ability, and is noted chiefly as a colorist." Despite my new-found-for-the-most-part-happiness, I was struck again and again by the meaninglessness of this creative activity. Why wasn't it going into new poems? At least I knew I could write. Or into something useful. Being a novice, an amateur, a *hobbyist* (not to mention a senior citizen) was un-nerving. The verbal part of my brain, that cool, critical and boring superego, attacked the colour-happy pleasure seeker. However, the speakerine was no match for the obsessive-compulsive now in control.

This shift in consciousness to the visual occurred after I'd decided not to do anymore overseas travel as a writer or anything of a public nature. Almost a Buddhistic withdrawal of identity, a test, and a risky move for someone with an unstable ego. I did experience moments of initiatory psychic jeopardy before the painting and collaging began.

When they began, *circles*—moons, suns, gongs, bicycle wheels—emerged as a dominant theme, especially in the collages. I started with a series called "Tibetan Desire" (a phrase from Leonard Cohen's *Beautiful Losers*) which featured a brass gong. The petroglyph bowl referred to in the title of my book, *Wilson's Bowl*, glowed, moon-bathed, through another sequence. Just recently I completed "The Greg Curnoe Cycle," all bicycle wheels and parts. Jung's spiritual mandala of maturity; Vaughan's "great ring of pure and endless light"; the Wheel of Fortune, life's cycle.

It's been an incredibly productive year in which I've acquired a little skill in painting, polish in the collages, and tennis elbow. Whether it's art as therapy or art as spiritual quest, the pursuit has given me back something like the pure vision I had as a child.

For the reader it might have been more interesting had I imagined achieving prime ministerhood, but that involved too much work. Besides, I've as little patience for what-might-have-beens as I have for nostalgia. From time to time, though, the deeper question of a former life twitches my sleeve. If the old Marxist materialist in me resists the idea of reincarnation, experience reveals in moments of vivid recall that I've had earlier existences. In India, for example. In Paris. And in a nineteenth-century dungeon where, in some manifestation, I lay, a political prisoner, decaying amid subdued ochres, umbers, brick-reds. Among these possible life contrivances is there an artist, brush in hand, painting a gong, a bowl, a spinning sun or wheel? In the land of only "what is" it hardly matters for—

> We are nothing; less than nothing; and dreams. We are only what might have been, and must wait upon the tedious shores of Lethe millions of ages before we have existence and a name.
>
> Charles Lamb, "Dream Children"

1994

Poetry and Psychobiography

Your shadow at morning striding behind you
Or your shadow at evening rising to meet you. . .

                                 T.S. Eliot, *The Wasteland*

·﹍

"My nerves are bad to-night. Yes, bad. Stay with me.
"Speak to me. Why do you never speak. Speak.
        "What are you thinking of? What thinking? What?
"I never know what you are thinking. Think."

This is T.S. Eliot speaking. In someone's voice. Whose voice? Whose?

I think we are in rats' alley
Where the dead men lost their bones.

That's another voice. Whose voice? Is that Tom Eliot's voice and the
first speaker's Vivian's, his wife? Vivian's "My nerves are bad tonight"?
Or mine?

We are in *The Wasteland*—the poem. To understand what's happening in the poem, it is not necessary to know Vivian's name or even that
Eliot had a wife, or that they were married on June 16, 1915, or that
their honeymoon in Eastbourne lasted only six days rather than the two
weeks planned, or that when they returned to London they stayed at
her family's house in Compayne Gardens in Hampstead, and afterwards
settled in for a while with Bertrand Russell in Bury Street, eventually
moving to 18 Crawford Mansions, or that Vivian took Bertie Russell to
bed. Once. Once too often for him—and no doubt for her too. All that
was before *The Wasteland* was written in 1921 and was Vivian still asking, if she ever did, in her "high parrot-like voice":

"What shall I do now? What shall I do?
"I shall rush out as I am, and walk the street
"With my hair down, so. What shall we do tomorrow?
"What shall we ever do?"

Russell thought her "light, a little vulgar, adventurous," though Eliot's biographer Peter Ackroyd interprets "vulgar" to mean "brash and high-spirited" because her unvulgar parents were an "exceedingly respectable upper-middle-class Edwardian couple." In any case, she was a good foil to Eliot, who could be "dull, dull, dull," or that's what Lady Ottoline Morrell thought when she first met the young man at Garsington in 1916. And then there were Vivian's gynaecological problems. What shall we do? What shall we ever do? Become sick, become writers (Mrs. Eliot wrote short stories, did you know?), go mad, become famous, lock up the wife in the loony bin. *But where are we?* Where did the poem go? "I think we are in rats' alley / Where the dead men lost their bones."

And I have led you here by devious means. This is Biography Alley, Microbiography Passage, Psychobiography Lane, though I can't seem to find them on the London map. And this is Lecture Freeway, and I must now say that Eliot had entirely something else in mind with his creepy rats' alley: "I will show you fear in a handful of dust," he wrote, that's what he wrote. In Part I of *The Wasteland*, "The Burial of the Dead."

Perhaps I, too, will show you fear in a handful of dust. Or just show you the rats. "I read, much of the night, and go south in winter."

·ᴗ

An American poet says to her psychiatrist: "Kafka, Dostoevsky are great because of the effect of their work. It's still going on; they are dead but it's still going on with the same impact as if they were alive. Their lives were messes, but it doesn't make any difference—what they *did* was more important than a good life."

How do I know what Anne Sexton, who committed suicide in 1974, said to her psychiatrist? I didn't know her; didn't know her friends; didn't know her psychiatrist. Wouldn't you think that what she told him in his office was privileged information and confidentiality an agreed-upon, though unsigned, contract? A bourgeois notion, some say, without which the Stasi, KGB, FBI, etcetera would wither away. While writing her excellent and sensitive biography of Anne Sexton, Diane Wood Middlebrook had access to over three hundred tapes of the poet's sessions with her psychiatrist, Martin T. Orne. Dr. Orne, with the approval of Sexton's daughter Linda (her literary executor), handed over this stash for what I must call the peak experience so far of psychobiography—though I use that term loosely at this point. Is there some significance in the fact that the first breach in publishing of the confidentiality rule that I know of occurred with a biography of a woman?

What could possibly justify this invasion of privacy? Sexton did talk about her writing to Dr. Orne—he was the one who suggested she start writing—and some of the quotations are useful in understanding her poetry and her relationships with other writers. Concerning her love affair with the poet James Wright, for instance, which began in earnest when Dr. Orne was in Australia and the affair was therefore interpreted by him as an acting out of transference, she said to her psychiatrist these not very flattering words:

> It makes transference to you seem like water to wine. He gives me so many gifts, but with both of us it's a "weird abun dance." Is it my mother—who is it? It doesn't have anything to do with sex [. . .] [discreet ellipses here on behalf of James]—he's not strong on responsibility—he's a genius—he makes me want to write. (134; first set of brackets in the original)

When Sexton's first book came out in 1960, *To Bedlam and Part Way Back*, the review she most took to heart was by James Dickey in *Poetry* (Chicago). Middlebrook writes:

> Sexton told Dr. Orne that she was mortified by Dickey's re mark that she wrote like an A student in the typical writing class. "But you've just started to write," her doctor observed. "I lack taste, I haven't had the real foundation," she countered. "This made me very original, because I'm really not up against a lot of things I have to imitate. Writ-

ing comes from inside, but you learn how to refine it. . . . As a poet, it may be better to be crazy than educated. But I doubt it." (126)

Those are interesting, if innocuous, quotes from the couch. But *Anne Sexton: A Biography* is also heavily loaded with the sort of material any psychiatrist's file would reveal: the family constellation, sexual abuse, and other behavioural aberrations, the intricate complexities of transference, suicidal obsessions, overdosing, and so on. Some of this material makes me cringe in embarrassment for Sexton and her family, but who knows if this flamboyant personality would have edited out of her biography, "by some enchantment," the many indecent exposures? She didn't leave a suicide note saying "Destroy the tapes!" as Virginia Woolf had instructed Leonard, or, rather, asked him "Would you destroy all my papers"—and a lot of good that did her. Let's see if I can justify the next quote as I continue my complicity with the biographer's eavesdropping.

On August 22, 1963, the year of Sylvia Plath's suicide, which produced a powerful effect on Sexton, Anne was scheduled to depart for Europe with a woman friend. Her anxieties increased as the date of departure approached. On the last day of July, Diane Middlebrook writes, "she had an especially dramatic session in Orne's office":

> Once in Dr. Orne's office, Sexton went directly to the air conditioner and began cradling it in her arms, then collapsed on the floor, where she spent the entire appointment curled up in a trance, ignoring Dr. Orne's voice, praying and calling him Nana. The next day she wrote a poem, "For the Year of the Insane," based on her inner experience of that hour. (201)

For the Year of the Insane

O Mary, fragile mother,
hear me, hear me now
although I do not know your words.
The black rosary with its silver Christ

90

lies unblessed in my hand
for I am the unbeliever.
Each bead is round and hard between my fingers,
a small black angel.
O Mary, permit me this grace,
this crossing over,
although I am ugly,
submerged in my own past
and my own madness.
Although there are chairs
I lie on the floor.

(131)

The issue of whether or not we should freight a work of art with extra-textual meaning and emotion is important and I'll return to it later.

The biographer did not take this opportunity to explicate the poem or refer to it any other way. Why do I feel that this particular scene is exploitative and the others are not? I suppose because Sexton's vulnerability is so crudely exposed and I have contributed to this invasion of privacy by quoting the passage in order to say that we have not earned such knowledge, and to say the obvious: that she has become a sociological phenomenon whose secret life has become an almost more dramatic gift than the poems, become the sacrificial meal we seem to hunger for.

•ᴗ

What is psychobiography and when did it begin? Ever since Freud hit on the idea of analyzing Leonardo da Vinci, biographers have been playing doctor, specialty psychiatry. Snooping in *The Freud / Jung Correspondence*, as I love to do, I found this Napoleonic manoeuvre in a letter from Freud to Jung, written in Vienna on October 17, 1909:

> I am glad you share my belief that we must conquer the whole field of mythology. . . . We need men for more far-reaching campaigns. Such men are so rare. *We must also take hold of biography* [emphasis mine]. I have had an inspiration since my return. The riddle of Leonardo da Vinci's character has suddenly be-

come clear to me. That would be a first step in the realm of biography. But the material concerning L. is so sparse that I despair of demonstrating my conviction intelligibly to others. I have ordered an Italian work on his youth and am now waiting eagerly for it. In the meantime I will reveal the secret to you. Do you remember my remarks in the "Sexual Theories of Children" to the effect that children's first primitive researches in this sphere were bound to fail and that this first failure could have a paralysing effect on them? Read the passage over. . . . Well, the great Leonardo was such a man; at an early age he converted his sexuality into an urge for knowledge and from then on the inability to finish anything he undertook became a pattern to which he had to conform in all his ventures: he was sexually inactive or homosexual. Not so long ago I came across his image and likeness (without his genius) in a neurotic. (255)

Well, it is, to say the least, cavalier—and demeaning, for the neurotic without genius and for the great Leonardo alike.

In England not quite ten years later, Lytton Strachey, in his 1918 Preface to *Eminent Victorians*, said of biographers: "With us, the most delicate and humane of all the branches of the art of writing has been relegated to the journeymen of letters; we do not reflect that it is perhaps as difficult to write a good life as to live one" (112). "Delicate and humane" are not adjectives one would readily apply to most psychobiographies, this sub-genre instigated by Freud, fallen upon by his colleagues in a form sometimes called pathography, brought into the literary mainstream by Strachey, sharpened much later by Erik Erikson as psycho-history, and then generalized and theoretically dispersed by innovators, though the party-liners are still with us to this day.

Strachey, with his wit and wickedness, and in a period when war had brought bitter home truths home, was peering into the mysteries of the human personality and seeing more than he felt he could tell his readers. But the hints are there. In the following passage from his brief life of the long-lived Florence Nightingale, I smell a sub-text. Florence had, it seems, a "calling" from an early age, but just exactly what was it?

Ah! To do her duty in that state of life unto which it pleased God to call her! Assuredly she would not be behind-hand in doing her duty; but unto what state of life *had* it pleased God to call her? . . . What was that secret voice in her ear, if it was not a call? Why had she felt from her earliest years, those mysterious promptings towards . . . she hardly knew what, but certainly towards something very different from anything around her? Why, as a child in the nursery, when her sister had shown a healthy pleasure in tearing her dolls to pieces, had *she* shown an almost morbid one in sewing them up again? Why was she driven now to minis-ter to the poor in the cottages, to watch by sick-beds, to put her dog's wounded paw into elaborate splints as if it was a human being? Why was her head filled with queer imaginations of the country house at Embley turned, by some enchantment, into a hospital, with herself as matron moving among the beds? Why was even her vision of heaven itself filled with suffering patients to whom she was being useful? So she dreamed and wondered, and taking out her diary, she poured into it the agitations of her soul. And then the bell rang, and it was time to go and dress for dinner. (112)

Oscar Wilde himself could not have done better with those sinuosities of tone. With suggestions of morbidity in little Florence's compulsion to heal, what a shower of reversals and criticism descends on the whole society, especially on the privileged class in which she was, as a young woman, trapped. What a clever set-up—so delicate, so witty, but humane? References to bed and sick-beds, insistence on God and the song-bird's soul, all those diseased and broken bodies lying around in the paragraph, and no reference at all to the Nightingale's own body—all this leads the reader to certain obvious conclusions.

Caught in the psychoanalytic undertow of this passage, I splash up against—can it be?—James? Yes, James, Lytton's brother, who just happens to be the translator of Freud's work into English. The first two volumes of *The Collected Works* will be published by Leonard and Virginia Woolf at their Hogarth Press in November 1921. James reminds me that Freud's paper on Leonardo da Vinci was translated and published in England way back in 1910. And Sigmund himself will, in far off 1928, write to Lytton to congratulate him on the "boldness and discretion" with which he applied the psychoanalytic method in his book *Elizabeth and Essex*, that is, in what he called the field of "psycho-history" (Edel, 255). (We must conquer the whole field of History, yes?)

By the 1930s psychoanalytic theory was indeed infiltrating history, and political science, and sociology, and social work, and medicine, and literary criticism, and biography. These disciplines were often to remain under the influence of classical Freudian theory longer than psychiatry itself for there the revisionist and empirical theories were developing which emphasized interpersonal and social dynamics and cure. In the 1940s and 1950s, I remember, the ideas of Eric Fromm, Harry Stack Sullivan, and Karen Horney were the subject of lively and heated discussions. In the course of time, more research, original theories, revisions and off-shoots have occurred, but in literary studies classical psychoanalytical theory has never gone away, as I'll show in a moment. However, the territory has opened up and most biographies today, though profoundly psychological, are not strictly speaking psychobiographies.

The model for psychobiography is clear and comes from a form Freud excelled at: the case history. Think of all those portraits, those unforgettable characters from Freud's writings: Dora, Little Hans, the Wolf Man, the Rat Man, Anna O. A case history, of course, is very limited in scope; it describes the course of treatment for a sick person, but biography is historical in perspective and sociological in texture, and the *work* of the artist is normally the reason for the interest in the life. The error of most psychobiography, it seems to me, is that the biographer sets up as physician/psychiatrist diagnosing some dread disease, without any hope of cure. The "patient" anyhow is usually dead, and the caring we associate with healing rarely comes into play. The case history as genre in the hands of a real doctor has recently taken on new life in the graceful, humane and delicate writings of the neurologist Oliver Sacks.

Another real doctor, Alma Halbert Bond, a psychoanalyst, provides me with a painfully funny example of the frailties of the psychobiographical method in its pure form as late as 1989. Dr. Bond has just been discussing an important passage in Virginia Woolf's novel *Between the Acts* and has said "that Woolf, like her playwright, Miss LaTrobe [of the novel], relied on affirmation from the outside world to counter-act feelings that her gifts were worthless. . . ." I won't give the whole paragraph, but Bond goes on:

> The history of Virginia's early toilet training could easily be re-corded in the above paragraph. Miss LaTrobe's pleasure in the giving of her gift may well parallel the infant Virginia's joy in presenting her mother or her nurse with her first fecal offerings. Like most individuals of that era, Mrs. Stephen probably did not understand her baby's strivings for mastery over the process of toilet training. In all probability, she did not realize that feces were her daughter's gift of love to her. So, Virginia, as many children, probably finished her first consciously directed bowel movement with a sense of failure and self-hatred that lasted all her life. (38-9)

Alma Bond's book is called *Who Killed Virginia Woolf? A Psychobiography*, and my answer would be you, in part, dear Alma Bond. By comparison, Louise De Salvo's biography, *Virginia Woolf: The Impact of Childhood Sexual Abuse on Her Life and Work* is almost scintillating in its theoretical and literary sophistication. Her book, published in the same year as Bond's, produces the now predictable result of turning another literary artist into a sociological product. But both of these works are benign when compared with the 1979 biography of Joseph Conrad by Frederick R. Karl. You may well be thinking by now that I'm proving nothing more than my resistance to psychological truths, but my resistance is even more interesting: I seem to be avoiding my topic tonight, "Poetry and Psychobiography." Well, I hope to get to it, but in my attempt to define psychobiography by these quotations, which I find too fascinating to relinquish for a mere topic, let me quote one more on a fiction writer in order to show the extreme cutting edge of the psychobiographical knife. At this point in *Joseph Conrad: The Three Lives*, Karl is discussing Conrad's wife's ailments:

> Jessie's ailments, whether knee, heart, or nerves, afforded her the rest she could not otherwise accept. Her condition shifted

the family fate to Conrad and gave her a respite. In their symbiotic relationship such additional pressure on Conrad allowed him to tighten his own screw and work better. Of course, the family situation that he was about to describe in *The Secret Agent* would hardly have been comforting to Jessie had she known what he was doing, or, later, had she applied it to her own family. For in that novel, already begun when Jessie became pregnant, was a perverse shattering of the family situation. Conrad was describing a group that cannibalized itself. With their father dead and their mother becoming senile, Winnie [of the novel] becomes the "mother" of her brother and, at the same time, takes on the father's role of holding the group together.

Every family tie is questioned or undermined, and then murder and suicide destroy all except the senile mother at the almshouse. In a figurative sense, Conrad the novelist has eliminated *his* family, which consisted of a much younger wife (as Winnie is with Verloc) and their child. By making Stevie retarded, Conrad revealed another aspect of hostility, a measure of retribution for the son [that is, Conrad's son] who must be supported and cared for. (591-92)

> *The Rat is the concisest Tenant.*
> *He pays no Rent.*
>
> Emily Dickinson, #1356

At first glance, one might see this sort of formulaic analysis as a failure to understand the profoundly deceptive nature of literature, which, like history, "has many cunning passages, contrived corridors, / And issues. . . ." (*The Wasteland*). Not so, says Roland Barthes: "All socio-ideological analyses *agree* on the deceptive nature of literature. . . ." Do practitioners of these methods see themselves, then, as the Thought Police of the pleasures of deception? At the mere mention of the words, "the pleasure of the text," says Barthes, "two policemen are ready to jump on you—the political policeman and the psychoanalytical policeman." Psychobiographer pigs have now, it seems, taken over from my psychobiographer rats. Pity.

If you've detected some rancour in my voice, I should confess that I, too, have been accused by a critic of "committing a murder disguised as a suicide," a conclusion drawn from a not too deceptive article I wrote for *Maclean's* many years ago. I've never figured out that one, nor have I ever completely recovered from the slander, which could explain my choice of topic tonight. Strangely enough, the subject presented itself to me only a day after I'd written a letter refusing to write a short autobiography, a task I found not only unpleasant but boring—meaning frightening. Is this talk, then, some urge to confess to the imagined crime after twenty years, or a very pleasant evening of revenge?

Speaking of revenge, have you perceived an anxiously influenced Oedipal struggle in these psychobiographers of the gratefully dead? You've seen how Freud toppled Leonardo, how Strachey tickled our fancy for belittlement, observed a hypothetical Virginia Woolf on her hypothetical potty, seen the dread knife applied to Conrad, and Anne curled up like a dog on the office carpet. How the dead men and women lost their bones. And yet Freud insisted, repeatedly, that "Before the problem of the creative writer, analysis must lay down its arms." "Its arms"—the conquistadorial image again. And is the creative writer really a problem? Obviously, there's some grand mystery surrounding the act of artistic creation that psychoanalysts and biographers feel compelled to penetrate. Freud believed that his space-probes into art and the lives of artists would reveal universal themes, themes of mythic proportions, and give him the opportunity to develop and advance his theories. His discoveries have perhaps justified his territorial ambitions in the field of culture, for who could now teach or study Sophocles, Shakespeare, or Dostoevsky without some reference to the Oedipus Complex and to Freud's writings on these culture heroes?

However, the influence is fading and psychiatry and psychotherapy have for years been shaking off the Freudian chains, and this relaxation is reflected in biography. I prefer, for instance, to read Diane Middlebrook on Sexton than Alma Bond on Woolf. By seeing Dr. Orne in our mind's eye at work with Sexton, we get a much better sense of process, rather than the author/patient as analog of a theoretical construct. We get more range with Jungian concepts coming in, Laingian permissiveness, Fritzian Perlsian you sit in my chair and I'll sit in yours dynamic, and much else.

Psychiatrists may not always deliver up the tapes, but more and more frequently they deliver up themselves for a chummy interview with the biographer in this new openness that so fascinates and appalls me.

Since Sylvia Plath died—that other glamorous American poet whose fame has flown on the broomstick of her suicide—several biographies have appeared, the most recent being *Rough Magic* by Paul Alexander (1991), which strikes me as being a clone of Anne Stevenson's *Bitter Fame*, though the two books have different hidden agendas. Stevenson quotes Plath's young and brilliant psychiatrist, Dr. Ruth Barnhouse (or Bleucher), as saying that when she gave Sylvia "permission to hate her mother . . . it went home like a shot of brandy." When Alexander interviewed Dr. B. she rattled on in what strikes me as a careless fashion:

> She wouldn't talk. She was furious. She was angry at her mother. She had too much plain living and high thinking—her words. She had been raised with this intense focus on the thinking function, on intellectual performance, which was not her nature. Using the Jungian categories of psychological types, she was an intuitive, feeling type; she just had an extremely high I.Q., that's all. (130)

Oh please! Throw in a childhood trauma or two, a few badly managed shock treatments, pharmaceutical overload. I'm sure this quote doesn't do justice to the psychiatrist because it's said she was quite successful with Plath, who did indeed have an extremely high I.Q.

For one more in the Jungian vein, I turn to H. F. Peters' study of Rilke's life and work, *Rainer Maria Rilke: Masks and the Man*—the title alone is promising, but as early as page twenty-nine I collide with this wave-like encratic bundle: Peters is discussing the poet's fragile identity:

> With Rilke, this dissolution of the ego went to dangerous extremes because he bestowed the energy belonging to positive thinking upon feeling sensation, which amounts to a reversal of the introverted type. When this happens [and here he is quoting Jung] "the qualities of the undifferentiated, archaic 'feeling-sensation' becomes paramount; i.e., the individual relapses into extreme relatedness, or identification with the sensed object." Jung calls this an *inferior extraversion*. (29)

The poems don't love us any more
they don't want to love us
they don't want to be poems
Do not summon us, they say
We can't help you any longer

Leonard Cohen (117)

My title, "Poetry and Psychobiography," arrived in the same way many titles of my poems arrive, by announcing itself. I wrote it down with that "Ah" feeling that comes with reading a good haiku. *Ah, that's it!* I wish I *had* written a poem, although that idea occurs to me only now as I type these words at a transitional crisis. I see the poem's shape appear before me—a broad poem on the page—and I know this is only page one—uneven lines, uneven margins, and, at the extreme right, halfway down, there's a shining blur fluctuating. While writing and thinking about this talk I've seen this golden light to the right just out there, but without the image of the poem. Possibly it's indicating a way out, possibly it holds within itself some kind of truth, or, if that's too big a word, then an insight or a surprise that I can't summon until I actually enter the incipient poem and gently approach that dazzle.

Poetic knowing is always in advance of the poet. A writer recently said to me, "Poetry has been my companion in my journey to myself, but it's always half a step ahead of me." Perhaps "journey" is too tame a word for this process: one step forward, two steps back is more like a mating dance between poet and poem. Feathers in full display, feet drumming the ground, the pair enacts a primal scene of creativity. One hopes the ritual in the sacred grove is protected by taboos as gift and grace are conceived. But then the psychobiographers, who always leave their dancing shoes at home, cut in, collapsing poet into poem, or poem into poet, carrying off their captive creature in triumph.

Off to the market place. The appetite among readers to read and biographers to write and publishers to publish biographies seems insatiable. I've little doubt that gossip and scandal these days count at the cash register. Profit alone could be a cynical rationalization for the use of the

Sexton tapes, for instance. But I don't think it's as simple as that, even if we add in the *People* magazine factor, and I'm afraid it's a real and gross factor, the urge to have the actor displace the act. Surely our desire to read these lives of the poets and other creative souls comes from a deeper source.

To deal with the Freudian possibilities first (to allay suspicions I'm afraid to deal with them), let me propose, in streaker fashion—a short dash naked through a public place—the "primal scene" theory, which I've just alluded to. Now with the reader in mind I'll rehearse this scene in the family drama, one of Freud's Ur stories, which begins when a child chances upon mother and father making love, or, to use a more clinical term, copulating, from the Latin *copulare*, to join or to link. What has been the missing link in the child's understanding of the parents' mysterious connection is revealed, for what it's worth, as violence, as rite, as animal physicality in which certain parts of the body are seen to have a function perhaps until now not understood. Parental authority is laid low; child is ascendant as voyeur, sometimes traumatized and burdened with guilt by this awesome scene, which is usually repressed. My argument, and it's not original I'm sure, is that in a sort of amnesiac repetition compulsion, the reader, like the criminal in a detective story, is compelled to return to the scene of the crime. Is this what's behind the blurb writer's curious and favourite description of a bestseller as "compulsive reading"?

This is done by opening the pages of a book, and another, and another. Let's say the one we're opening right now just happens to be a literary biography—psycho- or otherwise. Are we, am I, going in for a reality check on Mom and Dad, or art and fame, or poetry and madness? Am I going in search of a role model? Shall I imitate life or imitate art? Am I hunting for wilderness tips on my own craft, my own story, my origins, the secret of life itself? Creation?

Copulation and creativity, that pair of terrible twins, are fatefully conjoined, either literally in reproduction or that act transmuted into metaphor and symbol. They usually operate in secret, in *private*; hence the horror of and fascination with the invasion of privacy, that specialty of the secret service, television journalism, and biography. Whether a reputation is destroyed (or made) matters little as the cameras turn, spy spies, or the biographer plays the tapes and spins theories. We, as readers, enjoy the sport. Narratizing is, according to Julian Jaynes and others, an aspect of consciousness itself. We narratize our own lives from minute to minute; we narratize sensory experience into shapely clusters or gestalts, to make sense, and making sense means structurally making story.

Biographers, bless them, have to make a good story out of a life, even an uneventful life, and they have to use all their resources as researchers, scholars, and writers to get things right. There are a lot of things to get right: drafts and manuscripts, letters, critical studies, recorded and printed interviews, photographs, all kinds of data stored in attics and archives and libraries; in coat-pockets, in graveyards, in church and municipal records, in educational and mental institutions; on tapes, and now on floppy disks. Local history, world events, and the cultural surround of the subject must be surveyed and conveyed, literary influences tracked; friends and professional acquaintances of the subject, wives, husbands, lovers, teachers, relatives living and dead, physicians, psychiatrists—all must be made to tell all. And countries, cities, villages, schools, houses, hideaways traversed and explored. The work itself, the novels, plays, poems, short stories, essays, must be studied with scholarly closeness in the hope of deepening understanding, or offering a new angle, a fresh interpretation. For, after all, the writer's *work* must surely be the reason for all this diligent activity. Mustn't it?

The biographer's motivation could be more transcendent. Keats thought that serious biography should read like a kind of allegory, Goethe that it could be a mirror held up to the reader. Deflecting our gaze from some imaginary primal scene, we might look into a biography to catch a reflection of our life and times. Or seek out an allegory, a moral lesson, from, say, a life of Oscar Wilde or Emily Dickinson, Lorca or Lowell, or Plath, to find a Rake's or a Pilgrim's Progress, the tragic hero's tragic flaw, the myth of the Eternal Return.

·ᴖ

I foolishly promised to return to the question of whether or not we should import into a poem extra-textual meaning. It's much too large a question to raise at the last minute, so another short streak.

The poem might be described, minimally, as a thing, an artifact, a piece of paper, or a complex air sounded by a voice. Given our propensity to narratize experience, it's almost impossible not to bring to our reading or listening associations that distract, that scatter our attention, blur or sharpen our focus. Even the faintest whiff of our presence could just possibly influence the poem in the same way the scientist influences the experiment.

In the 1940s and 1950s the New Critics, as they were called—in the U.S. they included the influential John Crowe Ranson, Cleanth Brooks, and Allen Tate—attempted to put a clamp on any reference to the poet's life in the interpretation of the poem (and other limitations as well). For scholarly purposes this had a freeing effect on the poem which could then exist in its carefully crafted thingness as a virtually closed, though ambiguously meaningful, linguistic, and symbolic system, user-friendly mainly to academics who had a knowing finger on the entry key.

In the intervening decades much has happened in thematics and schematics. I find it interesting that while the deconstructionists have been in the ascendant biographies have proliferated and the biographers, who tend to be generalists, though there are fine critics too, have grown more and more psychological in their approach to the life and works of their subjects. Now another important group of academic critics, once again mainly American, has appeared whose "urgent business is cultural history." They are the New Historicists. Now this sounds like comfortable territory for the growing tribe of literary biographers. In a neat condensation of some of the underlying principles of the New Historicism, Frank Kermode, in the *New York Review of Books*, quotes Stephen Greenblatt ("the chef d'école" and author of *Shakespearean Negotiations: The Circulation of Social Energy in Renaissance England*, 1988): "[W]orks of art, however intensely marked by the creative intelligence and private obsessions of individuals, are the product of collective negotiation and exchange." Kermode continues:

> Accordingly he means to explore "the poetics of culture"—to study the "half-hidden cultural transactions through which great works are empowered." So instead of treating Shakespeare's plays as somehow isolated or autonomous, he will seek to show how they benefit

from the "social energy" they derive from their "negotiations" with other aspects of culture. For, like people, these works are to be thought of as products of what Foucault calls the "dynamic circulation" of social discourses. (43)

If the utilitarian New Historicists—who may sometimes borrow a precision tool from the deconstructionists or micro-historians—if they take all culture as their urgent concern, then the social discourses are many, the negotiations more than bilateral, and the work of art is in danger of being de-aestheticised, domesticated, drained of pleasure. Well, that's life.

Psychoanalysis and psychiatry have been dominant social discourses in the twentieth century, influencing almost all disciplines and all the arts. If poetry thinks it can escape this social energy then, like the Dead Sea Scrolls before they were discovered, poetry should seal itself up in a time capsule and blast off from Cape Canaveral. *Do I contradict myself? Very well then I contradict myself*, as Walt Whitman so bravely said before me. There they go! Leonard Cohen's poems blast off in a huff: "Do not summon us," they say, "We're too beautiful for words and we hate the cops. We can't help you any longer." Leonard was probably in a blue funk the day the poems talked back—

HURRY UP PLEASE IT'S TIME. HURRY UP PLEASE IT'S TIME.

What's this? Who said that? My God, a monster Time Machine has just swooped down to take me on a last minute magical mystery tour. What shall I ever do? Where am I? Ah—it's the Palatine Gallery of the Pitti Palace in Florence, circa 1895, and there's André Gide with his splendid profile. He looks so young! He's studying a painting by Giorgione; it's called, I think, *Concert.* He steps back, takes me by the elbow and points to the painting, says with all the assurance of youth, "In front of this painting you think of nothing else, and that is characteristic of a masterpiece." I'm disarmed by the charming French accent and can only weakly say, "Would you please repeat that?" "*In front of this painting you think of nothing else,* and that is characteristic of a masterpiece." Before I can say "j'y suis, BUT WHAT ABOUT POETRY?" I'm gone (Gide, 45-6).

I'm in Paris—ah, gay Paree. I'm in Rainer Maria Rilke's flat where he's at his writing table, illumined by a small golden bowl of light, Rilke, my spiritual guide and mentor (one good narcissist deserves another). I'll just creep up behind dear Rainer and see what he's writing. A letter, 1903. To Lou Andreas Salomé. He must have just come back from the Louvre, for I think he's writing about examples of ancient art, *anonymous* art, that power:

> No one knows what their intention is . . . no subject is attached to them, no irrelevant voice interrupts the silence of their concentrated reality, and their duration is without retrospect or fear. . . . The masters from whom they originate are nothing; no misunderstood fame colors their pure forms; no history casts a shadow over their naked clarity—! *They are.* (Rilke, 303)

As I try to slip away from his luminous presence, his concentrated reality, I'm swept off my feet again and dropped down into gloomy old, foggy old London town. An underground office in Lloyds Bank. A tall, lean figure paces up and down chanting *Shantih shantih shantih.* Strangely familiar, but what does it mean? Of course, it's Mr. Eliot writing poetry on company time: *The Wasteland,* 1921. He senses my presence, twirls around. "You!" he accuses, "You!" fixing me with his baleful eyes. If you ask me, he looks like a man on the verge of a nervous breakdown. "You—nattering on about Vivian's bedding Bertie Russell and Ottoline's silly gossip!" And then he points, and not like André; this time the finger points at me! He intones in that sepulchral voice:

> *Your shadow at morning striding before you*
> *Or your shadow at evening rising to meet you;*
> *I will show you fear in a handful of dust.* (50)

1993

Phyllis Webb's Canada

In August 1969, an artist called Vazan drew a crescent line by walking along a sandy beach at low tide in Victoria, P.E.I., while another artist walked a similar line along the British Columbia shores. "Of course," said Vazan, "when the tide changed, the water erased my crescent line, but for a whole day we had Canada in parentheses." When I read that story in the newspaper something joyfully tumbled over in me. Those wild men on the beaches (from sea to shining sea) had made a witty, imaginative, sardonic statement about Canada, and they'd created, if not art, at least an event. It was an event of the imagination and therefore magical.

It went beyond a spoof of those familiar word-assemblages, such as International Pewter (Canada) Limited and the economic and political realities they represent. It went beyond the dictionary definition of "parenthesis": *a word, clause, sentence inserted into a passage to which it is not grammatically essential* (apply that one to Canada and it's pretty devastating). Canada is a whole bundle of parentheses, and emotionally we are all caught in the embrace of those inhibiting arms. Even Canada's role as mediator in international disputes can be seen in terms of this image. The magic of the event was the psychological revelation that once we see, feel, and make external the bind we're in, the tides can come in and wash it away. (The tides can also come in and wash *us* away.)

I wonder if many Canadians share the secret ambition I had to be buffeted by the Atlantic and prevail against the winds off the Pacific. It took a few years and a little good luck to get from St. John's, Newfoundland, to Long Beach, British Columbia. Just to feel the limits of the land. To be at the extremes.

I've settled, temporarily, for island waters and quiet, parenthetical ways. Salt Spring Island on the west coast is a good place for star-gazing and navel-gazing, a nice shy corner of the universe which doesn't clamour for recognition or glory. A good place, maybe, for getting a perspective on life and times.

To put my Canada in perspective, I find I have to put myself in perspective. Line up the labels and mix the metaphors. It's not much fun. Now in early middle-age, I find myself more rebellious, more radical, less patient, often in despair at the insanity of our life, from which I believe I'm saved by profound public and personal angers. I'm disaffected from my governments, even from the process of government, and from many of the institutions of the society which formed me. I've become a snarling writer of letters-to-the-editor, which I never write, a supporter of causes I never join. I am a voter who has never voted for a winning candidate, and a law-abiding anarchist. No party would have me if they knew what I really think. I won't have any of them because I know what they really think. Spiritually, I'm French-Canadian separatist; in fact and in flesh a pure-bred west coast WASP. I'm a card-carrying Canadian (and a very useful card it is too). Made in Canada, it says.

As I sit here brooding on this nest of paradoxes—lay it on the line, Phyllis, lay it on the line—I am confronted by what is for me the best of all possible worlds. Today I can watch from my window the sea shifting from cobalt blue to dove grey. The cliché seagulls make little white sun reflectors out in the harbour; trees on the tiny Three Sisters islands are a cold, green resting place for the eyes. The ferries of Mr. Bennett's navy push on to Active Pass, moving whitely and stately through the Strait of Georgia. A study in blue, white, green, grey. And when the tide goes out I can gather oysters. C'est mon pays. It's my country.

But what is "my Canada"? This best and very temporary world on a Gulf Island is just a corner, and I don't own an inch of it. I don't possess any real estate. My Canada is unreal estate, a fantasy that changes as I change. I can't fix it.

When I was a schoolgirl in Victoria, B.C., there was that big event, the coronation. Not Elizabeth! King George the Sixth. I remember the coronation mugs that became a part of the household china, though I don't remember how we got them at school, or why. I remember flapping my hand at the King and Queen as they drove through the streets of the city "when they came to visit us." I suppose that's part of my Canada. It's a vivid memory. The weather was fine. But I think I became a Canadian and claimed my country when I was seventeen and arrived at political consciousness. That sense of being a Canadian was later amplified and made more subtle by a literary consciousness and a general broadening of my horizons.

These things came to pass not in the airy rafters of my brain alone, but in places, and the places are all mixed in with love, friendships, food, seasons, poems, neurosis and nonsense. I could name you streets, · restaurants, hotel rooms, beaches, grassy nooks, class rooms, and bus routes that are as much my Canada as Capital Hill or the mountain ranges of the west coast. But I'm not writing a novel.

When I was seventeen, the war had not yet burned and blasted to a halt. I suppose when my social science teacher trundled her chicks off to the B.C. legislature she didn't know the trip was going to hatch two teenage "radicals" and that four years later I would be running in a provincial election, the youngest candidate ever fielded at that time, for the CCF. In 1945, the CCF had been demanding, among other things, votes for Asiatics and native Indians. That plank in the party platform was for me a springboard, and I jumped in. In 1949 the CCF ran the first Indian candidate. He won. I lost. (Losing is one of the important experiences in the life of a Canadian, but there's no need to make a habit of it.) So at that time I was beginning to identify the needs of this country and project a vision of what it could be.

I can still see a Sikh temple on a high hill in Victoria where I gave a campaign speech. The beautiful women in their saris—saffron, green, plum, cerise—on one side of the temple; the handsome men in their turbans on the other; a great bird-like fan above my head, an interpreter by my side. And the gnawing thought that "we had their vote."

I've skated over some pretty thin ice in my time, but when I first walked on water I knew I'd finally made the Canadian scene. Before I moved to Quebec, I'd never seen a large body of water frozen so hard trucks could drive over it. When I walked on Lac St. Louis at Ste. Anne de Bellevue, I understood something about miracles. A poem began steaming out on the cold air, "Almost a Jesus, I walk on waters white with a white stride . . ." Yes, this was really Canada! Snow, ice, freezing rain, trees draped in icicles, pristine, dazzling against a blue sky. In Quebec, each season was a challenge. Winds and drifts in winter; heat and humidity in summer; spring sprang out like a green lion, and autumn was almost too beautiful to bear. It was a challenge, but after a few strenuous years I realized the climate was a form of natural madness and fled.

Each of my self-imposed exiles—to England, France and the U.S.—ended in return. Now I'm a permanent resident. Why?

One day in Paris, sitting in a café downing one more *grog*, I came up with a new punning name for myself: I was a Parisite. With my limited talents, I could only feed off France. I felt I wanted to do more with my life than be a parasitical guest at a gourmet feast. A remnant of the Puritan ethic still numbed my taste-buds. Then there was language. As a poet I could only write in English if I wanted to say what I meant. And as a *Canadian* poet I had access to a network of poet-friends across the country who were nursing an infant unicorn called Canadian Poetry. I wanted to help the dainty monster grow.

Maybe it was all much simpler than that. Maybe I kept coming back because it was simply home.

In Canada, I've worked as a cookie-packer, a waitress, a cashier-hostess, a secretary. I've been a teacher, a broadcaster, and on the staff of CBC Public Affairs. And, throughout all, for love not money, I have tried to write poetry. I've done these things in Victoria, Vancouver, Montreal, and Toronto. That route and all the people on it have been my life-line to the experiences of being Canadian.

Right now, I'm afraid for my country, not because Quebec might separate (that might force us into some useful original thinking), but because so many Canadians don't give a damn about their freedom. They rock in the cradle of the Great Parentheses, sucking their thumbs, humming an old tune, "Law and Order." So what if Vancouver Mayor Tom Campbell threatens to round up hippies and draft resisters under the War Measures Act? Vote him in for another mindless term. So what if innocent people in Quebec are jailed? A good place to think. (It certainly is.) So what if you can be retroactively guilty? *C'est la vie.* As a professional non-joiner, I've done a very amateurish thing. I have become a member of the B.C. Civil Liberties Association. That may seem like a very pathetic gesture, but it is the kind of gesture most Canadians of my generation are still capable of acting out without embarrassment or humility.

Last summer, shortly after I had come to the island, I received a letter from a young man—I presume he was young—telling me to "get lost." And why? Because I wasn't, he thought, writing about Canadian problems in my poems. This seems to me to be carrying the new nationalism a bit far. Anyhow, I'm not 100 percent Canadian content, as a person or poet, and I fear anyone who is. It's a question of relative values. Once again William Vazan leaps out of the headlines to help me make my point: "Artist Draws a Line Across Canada—Why?" Vazan answers, "It all comes out of the idea that the world is shrinking. The line will mark space and distance, elements that have been changed so much by things like moon landings that they don't mean what they used to mean." It was probably fun getting eight galleries across the country involved in taping Canada, but with a few words I put it more bluntly. Canada is not the belly-button of the world. Nor, thank God, is it the panic-button. If I'm grateful for anything I'm grateful for that.

If I say my Canada is unreal estate, that is a personal and idiosyncratic way of saying time passes, the pictures change, and we will always be dreaming up new pictures for new futures. It is also a way of indicating where the *real* estate is. I find it helpful to think that "my" corner of Canada this minute, with its cobalt sea, is an infinitesimal part of the globe, and I am aware of this every time I switch on the news or watch the sun come up. The Earth is our real estate, our terribly threatened royal domain.

I often think that in our search for a Canadian identity we fail to realize that we are not searching for definitions but for signs and omens. The ancients used to read the entrails of sheep; we keep reading our own entrails and end up with ulcers. I'm not good at book history, at dates and the chronology of events that surround the Macdonalds and Browns and Lauriers, to speak only of Canada. But recently I have been going into a different past for a few lessons. I have been studying stones. The rock art of the Indians of British Columbia has been neglected in favour of the more dazzling (and portable) wood carvings, like totem poles and masks. Today I received a letter from a friend who shares my enthusiasm for petroglyphs and who has seen them in many parts of the world. She had just been to visit a recently discovered and relatively unknown site on Vancouver Island, and she writes: " . . . a huge ceremonial place, most of which is probably still to be discovered. There are many styles and probably periods, but the design and workmanship are beautiful beyond belief. The water from above was running across carvings of sea snakes and eels and the effect, which I am sure was intentional, is one of rich marine life swimming. A Chinese dragon of a beauty I have never seen anywhere, the hermaphrodite crouching on top of it all reminding me of something I have seen before—a Maya glyph? Two dancing figures, one beautifully masked, almost Egyptian, the other with a huge phallus, the legs like a Buddhist statue, big feet. . . . There seems to be a definite relation to the sun, which hit the figures from the west head on and made them dance, all facing east down slope. The whole site must have been worked, levelled, polished. . . . "

The site may well be pre-Canadian, but geographically it lives at my back door. It adds a dimension to the pastness of where and how I, a Canadian, live. It beckons me into its wisdom. Soon I shall go and see it and try to read the signs and omens of those figures dancing for the sun. I think they will have something to say. (I may even find some Canadian content.)

1971

A Correspondence

When at last I got all the way there,
what I found was myself coming back.
> Wilson Duff, "Spirit Quest"

But what about the 'burning desire' to contact the author? The author:
pseudonym? anonymous? amorphous? intangible? You would only be
contacting yourself.
> Wilson Duff to Lilo Berliner
> 20 August 1973

I think terror and pain activate equations—and hunger and laughter.
> Lilo Berliner to Wilson Duff, 14 June 1975

Early in 1973, Lilo Berliner, a reference librarian at the University of Victoria, wrote to Wilson Duff, a well-known anthropologist and professor at the University of British Columbia, requesting permission to xerox one of his papers, "Levels of Meaning in Haida Art."[1] Lilo was passionately interested in Northwest Coast Indian art, particularly petroglyphs—Indian rock carvings. It was because of my own new discovery of petroglyphs in 1970 that I was introduced first to Lilo Berliner and then to Beth Hill, who was working on her book *Indian Petroglyphs of the Pacific Northwest.* Duff had sent Beth Hill his "Levels of Meaning" and she had shown it to Lilo. This strange network of connections was to affect all our lives in ways we could not foresee.

Lilo, a German-born American, widely travelled and multilingual,

---

This essay, written in 1977, was originally destined for a memorial volume on the late Professor Wilson Duff, anthropologist, to be published by the British Columbia Provincial Museum. The editorial committee eventually decided to withdraw it as unsuitable in the context of the other presentations. I now agree with that decision, seeing, as Wilson Duff's daughter saw, that the essay is rather more focussed on Lilo Berliner than Duff. I would like to thank Marnie Duff for permission to publish these extracts from her father's letters.

had followed the petroglyph and pictograph trail from Alaska to South America. She was a seeker after signs and symbols. Given to Zen-like insights and absurdities, she was also addicted to Jungian archetypes, dreams, and synchronicities. I have not yet decided exactly what it was in Wilson Duff's "Levels of Meaning" that attracted her so powerfully. Lilo's intelligence was essentially poetic and her impulse mystical, and it is possible that his statement, "Iconics is the language of metaphor in art, opening the way to the full use of metaphor as a method of cognition," had a particular resonance for her. However, I think it was something more diffuse and pervasive: Wilson's "passionate reticence," his search for meaning and pattern, and his perception of an "advanced mathematics" in Haida art.[2] Perhaps she even guessed that this was all part of his own Spirit Quest and matched her own. Although Lilo Berliner could perceive the poetics of an advanced mathematics, she preferred the calculus of "the full use of metaphor as a method of cognition" for her own pursuits.

Their correspondence, which began in 1973 and continued until late 1975, is fascinating as a dialogue between two persons who never met and yet could share ideas, intuitions, feelings, secrets, and jokes. In his letters Wilson explored his way into his theories of paradoxes and equations which he would advance in *Images Stone b.c.: Thirty Centuries of Northwest Coast Indian Sculpture*, the catalogue for an exhibition originating at the Victoria Art Gallery in March 1975. These theories were to make Wilson Duff a controversial figure in British Columbia anthropology. He felt Lilo in her intuitive way understood him best. But in 1974 he began to send poems, his own and those of a young Indian woman from the Tlingit region, and his letters, as such, decreased. Lilo's increased. There are seventeen Duff letters extant and twenty-four Berliner letters. All are typed, except one card and one short note from Lilo and a postscript by Wilson. The correspondence began in January 1973; Wilson's last letter was written in June 1975 and Lilo's in December of the same year.

In April 1975, Lilo retired from the University of Victoria library, prematurely, but just in time to devote herself wholly to the "Images" exhibition, which she visited four times in Victoria and twice in Vancouver. She then travelled to Colorado and Arizona to continue her study of rock art. In August 1976, Wilson Duff committed suicide. In September 1976, Lilo moved from Victoria to Salt Spring Island where she would be shown and take possession of a small bowl, or basin, carved into a rock on the beach near her "Zen house" which she rented from Beth and Ray Hill. She immediately dedicated it to Wilson and called it "Wilson's bowl." Incredibly delicate, perfectly round, empty at low tide, full at high, it reflects the moon with calculated magic. It was the perfect object for her contemplation of levels of meaning. In January 1977, thinking of the bowl, of Wilson, "my twin," and having plotted with the full moon, she walked into the sea.

•ﾉ

When Wilson sent Lilo his permission to copy "Levels of Meaning" (5 February 1973), with its Bill Reid cover design, he wrote, "it's funny, but I don't want that paper widely read. I have the feeling, which maybe isn't completely true, that I have come a million miles since then."[3] Perhaps to indicate the direction in which he was going, he enclosed "a little Haida Christmas story" because "you are such a friendly and perceptive person." Not yet understanding Lilo's ability to gather all and anything into her symbolic system, he added, "I cannot quite see how my approach applies to petroglyphs, as I am dealing mostly with a system of brush painting almost as complicated as Chinese calligraphy. Power to you anyway."

The little Haida story was called "Nothing Comes Only in Pieces." Lilo, who was always on the alert for the Zennish sound of one hand clapping, on receiving this gift, clapped the other, sang out Yes! Yes! and on 20 February wrote:

> With your position paper, your stimulating letter, and "Nothing Comes Only In Pieces" in front of me, would it be crude to quote you and say that they opened "a mind stretching pattern of awareness," which has made me incredibly happy during the last few weeks. In fact, I have hesitated writing before because your comments on our ability and inability to see nothing, to experience real laughter, to see the beginning in the end and the end in the beginning [all this being contained in "Noth-

ing. . ."] have somehow complemented my readings in Suzuki, Jung, the Popol Vuh, lately Lévi-Strauss' *L'Homme Nu*. The philosophy, the visual experience and the literary form one magnificent whole. I am playing with the idea of a Circle. In any case I can carry it from petroglyphs, northwest painting, the Chinese calligraphy you mentioned, Eskimo prints right through to Henry Moore and Barbara Hepworth. What a fine game on so many levels!

On 25 May, Wilson Duff sent a revision of the "Nothing. . ." story. He explained how he wanted it to be published, and "also, I want it illustrated by the use of one chest design (the one in my earlier paper) with certain parts 'lifted out' to reveal without words the solution to one of the most stubborn puzzles of the Northwest Coast." It is possible Bill Reid will know this problem and its solution. And just as possible that only Wilson Duff ever knew it.

Because the "Nothing. . ." story is a ground theme and reference point in these letters, I will indicate as briefly as possible its salient features. Nothing may come only in pieces, but this Raven creation myth, the story's core, comes whole, from J. R. Swanton:

> In the earliest times, a boundless expanse of sky overspread a boundless expanse of sea. In the sea lay a single reef, on which all the supernatural beings were heaped together, asleep. Raven flew about above the sea, unable to find a foothold; and at last, looking at the neighbouring sky, he became fascinated by it. Then he ran his beak into it and climbed up.
>
> In the sky-country lay a five-row town, where the chief's daughter had just given birth to a child; and when night came, Raven entered the chief's house, scooped the baby out of its skin, and took its place. The infant was not old enough to receive any substantial nourishment: so Raven became hungry, and, slipping out at night, stole an eye from everyone in one row of the town, and these he ate. He did this four nights in succession. A woman who was stone from her hips down, and who never slept, sat in one corner of the house, however, and

observed what was happening. At last she told the people.

Then the town chief called the people together, and they sang a song for the child. In the midst of it, however, the one holding it let it fall, and it dropped down out of the sky country, turning to the right in its descent, until it fell upon the surface of the great waters. Now the cradle drifted about a long time, and the child cried a long time, until it cried itself to sleep; but while it slept, something said, "Your powerful grandfather invites you in." Raven turned quickly towards the sound, but there was nothing there. By and by the same thing happened. Then he looked through the eyehole in his marten skin blanket, and presently out from beneath the water came a grebe, which said, "Your powerful grandfather invites you in."

Then it dived out of sight. Now Raven got up, and he found his cradle floating against a kelp with two heads. He stepped on it, and, lo! it was really a two-headed house-pole made of stone. When he clambered down, he found he could get along as well as in the air.

Beneath was a house, and, as he stood before it, a voice came from it saying, "Come inside, my son; I hear that you come to borrow something from me." Now Raven entered, and in the back part of the house sat a man with hair as white as a seagull. Then the old man sent him for a box which hung in the corner. There were four others inside of this, and, pulling them apart, he took out two long objects—one covered with shining points; the other black. Handing them to Raven, he said, "I am you. That is you." He referred to some slender blue objects walking about upon the screen in the rear of the house.

Then the old man said, "Lay this speckled stone in the water first, and last this black one; after which bite off a piece of each and spit it out again, and the pieces will reunite. But when Raven had gone out, he put the black one into the water first; and when he had bitten off part of the rock with shining points and spit it out again, the pieces rebounded. He had done differently from the way he had been told.

Now he went back to the black one, bit off part of it and

spit it out again, when the pieces stuck. These were going to become trees. He put this into the water, and it stretched itself out, becoming the Haida country, to which all the supernatural beings swam over.

This core of "Nothing Comes Only In Pieces" is conveyed by means of a somewhat simplistic device: a young teacher from Vancouver, "straight out of the University," wanting to inject some Native culture into the curriculum of her school in the Charlottes, begins by telling this myth to the class. Since it presents problems that neither she nor any of the Indian students in the class understand, she asks one of them, Ray Wilson, to inquire of "Chini" Solomon Wilson about some of the puzzling elements of the story. This he does in what turns out to be a sort of Haida Socratic dialogue, to produce a vernacular exegesis of this creation myth which, because of its particular paradoxes, Wilson Duff found compelling.

In an explanatory note to the story, Duff writes, "The Creation Myth as mimeographed by the teacher comes straight out of Swanton's 'Contributions to the Ethnology of the Haida' (1905a, 72-74). Swanton published the same myth in a slightly longer and less edited form in 'Haida Texts and Myths, Skidegate Dialect' (1905b, 110-112). The corrections Sol makes on the basis of 'the way John Sky told it to me' are mostly from that version. Solomon Wilson lives at Skidegate, and although I know him quite well, I have not discussed myths with him."

Some of the details which Ray and Chini Sol dwell on in the story include: why are there five boxes instead of four, usually a mystical number among the Haida? The significance of the eyes; the birth and personhood/ spirithood of Raven ("he was only an intention?"); the meaning of the half-rock woman; the nature and meaning of "the two long objects," the stones Raven took from the innermost box; and the significance of the size and emptiness or fullness of that box. Here is just a sample on the Nothing theme:

> "I was thinking about those two things in the box. One of them was that tiny little nothing that was there but was too small to have any size, so the box looked empty. You know what I think

the other thing was, Sol? It was all the other things in the world that were not there, so the box still looked empty. You see, if you mixed them. . . ."

Sol's guffaw brought that line of reasoning to a halt. "You and your crazy ideas, Ray. That's sure a crazy one." They laughed together. "But you know, Ray, that old man did say that nothing comes in pieces, so at least it's something you can have a piece of, something that Raven could have a bite of. Maybe that's how it is: you can't see nothing when it's all there, you can only recognize it when there's a little piece of it there."[4]

Two important "adumbrations" in the exegesis are Haida proverbs offered by Chini Sol as partial answers to the ontological questions he (read Wilson Duff) finds in this particular Creation Myth. These are "The world is as sharp as a knife," and "Nothing Comes Only In Pieces" ("I guess I made up the title"—Duff). Wilson later came to think of them as an equation, as "Duff's Law."

As I have been preparing this paper I have found myself asking two questions regarding the story. First, why, with his inclination for Freudian interpretations, Wilson did not suggest the "two long objects" found in the innermost box were twins? Answer? He had not yet seen the great twin stone masks *nested* together (but see Duff letter, 3 June 1975). Second, why didn't Wilson refer, even in a passing aside by his character Chini Sol, to the myth in which Raven finds the moon (or the sun) in the innermost box of a *ten*-box set, which would have given strength to the need for five boxes in the Creation Myth and added delicious mathematical and symbolic complications. Answer? It does not offer the same perspective on Nothing, since it is not a Creation Myth; and Raven is in no way confused about what to do with the moon (or the sun?). In either case, the boxes are certainly all stacked in his favour.

In a letter to Lilo, 10 March 1974, Wilson was still absorbed in his chosen myth, his attention now focussed on time:

The events in the myth, although strung along a single line of narrative time, do not all happen in the same frame of time. Down below, I think, time is not moving. It is the non-time between death and re-birth. Things happening there are happening in two times at once in the sense of "in sequence but not in time." . . . Implicit oneness. Alternate bites of that are what the world is made of. Alternation in time.

. . . Just for fun, though, I suggest that you take the events of the myth which occur in the sky world, and run the sequence *backwards*, to see what logic, if any, appears, and to help me look for the way in which the end and the beginning meet in the middle and find themselves the same.

Lilo was a willing student, if not always a disciplined one. She used to say that her letters to Wilson were automatic writing, or that she was sleep-walking on the typewriter keys. She conveyed the sense of behaving like a naughty child who relished the professorial response which Wilson sometimes offered. Her replies were often provocatively non-linear, associative, and dream-like, but I am sure Wilson detected the inner logic and enjoyed the casual, absurdist, at times abandoned approach. Her first attempt at running the sequence backwards was written on 16 March 1974:

The middle is the box. The middle of the outer box is the last inner box. In getting there you find the Way. The Way has many dimensions or levels, somewhat like a maze or labyrinth, only much more intricate, combining those with the Chinese puzzle. . . . You begin by the process by which it makes itself known. . . . I woke up and thought of the box. I realized you had become the box. . . . I thought you had become the box in the Zen way. . . . Have I met Raven? I can't wait to get back to the box, or out to the beach, which is probably the same thing.

On 23 March, she pulled herself together and tried again:

Your letter backwards. The little hole which Raven dug to put the eyes in is the center, I think. If I start the story backwards, it goes something like this. Raven flew up from the surface of the great waters. The sky people sang a song for him. He was given to the chief's daughter (or the chief's daughter found him which seems to be what usually happens. In fact she could hide him). He digs the hole. He spits out something, mixes it with ashes and makes eyes. He gives an eye to each of the one-eyed sky people. Having done this he returns to the sea. (Or perhaps the sky people got their third eye to give them the wisdom associated with sky people).

And then, as if she had done her lesson, she takes flight:

> In fact, out of the smallest box came the Big Bang and the Static State theories. The Big Bang may just be the popping sound of Raven eating the eyes.[5] A friend who is a T'ai Chi enthusiast says that just before the end of the sequence there is a sound made by slapping one's toes. That is the only sound in all the movements. When you reach the end, the whole sequence can be done backwards. I have also thought briefly of the Central American ball courts and the strange, unexplained rings (are these other boxes?) and the ball, which I think was considered the sun or the moon, but could just as well be the eye ball.
>
> The complete eye can be considered as window, facing in and out, or as mirror. The eye socket as female principle, the cup or vessel. The eye ball as male principle (I think this is wrong) [not according to Freud] and I had not thought of it until now. It would be better to think of it as spirit, like the Holy Ghost in the trinity. I seem to be very Christian today. Also I am not very bright and I have already revealed too much of that. It is strange how everything has become just another aspect of the creation myth, and I am enclosing a Henry Moore article from a recent "Listener."

Before the box game was over, however, Wilson wrote Lilo a long letter on Christmas Eve 1973, which was "the best gift I have ever received in my 52 years. It should last a lifetime." The letter, reproduced here in part, was indeed a tightly packed Christmas box:

> I have the feeling that I have finally cracked the code, and have found the trail that will lead to understanding the great things

the Edenshaws were doing. I have gone beyond "Levels of Meaning" . . . and found another way in which the art was working. It involves paradoxes, like the box paradox in "Nothing." . . . It often makes uses of pre-existing structural oppositions in the shapes of artifacts to state equations which are at the same time paradoxes (on a spoon, handle is to bowl as piercer is to container and as ultimate-piercer is to ultimate-engulfer). It has a complicated vocabulary of images to work with (. . . and as Raven's beak is to Bear's mouth). It plays with inversions of part and whole, literal and figurative, present and absent, explicit and implicit. It is always trying to find new images for the two hands of God.

The main thing the art seems to be saying is "I control paradox" (with whatever follows from that). It seems to work with some of the paradoxes which are hidden and implicit in myths (to a certain extent, Haida art is a structural analysis of Haida myth). If there is a paradox which it cannot control, it creates another paradox to cancel it out by producing the same result. One example is the paradox of Creation, which the mind creates by postulating an initial nothingness out of which the world emerges. But how can something be formed out of nothing? The Haida answer was to construct another intertransformation of two opposite things into each other. Raven, in the fact of being born, brings into existence his own mother. A process, creating its own antecedents and its own consequences, both at the same time. Needless to say, in this system there is no "beginning of time," there only exists the present moment. There is no creation, there is only transformation. Opposites, intertransforming into each other.

This cannot be clear without a lot of examples. But I think you will know intuitively that something is there.

The examples would marvellously present themselves in two years with the "Images" exhibition, but Lilo did understand, intuitively and without examples:

At first reading I laughed to myself and shouted yes, yes, yes! This morning the same. There were four black oyster-catchers and one gull on the rock outside the window to confirm it. To-night the brightest sky with the quarter moon. I dare not say I understand it, although I think I do, completely and with great joy. It must be intuitive, as you say, for I certainly do not have the necessary background.

. . . Considering my own state of excitement and joy, I can-not visualize yours—the impact of search, find and expression must be like the systematic creation of a miracle, making you the transformer. Yet your letter seems so calm on the surface. (29 December 1973)

And Wilson, 10 March 1974:

Dear Lilo: I think of you often, and of your response to my last letter, and wonder how it could be that you, more than anybody else, have caught so much of the glory and elation of the re-awakening of Edenshaw's system of thought.

What I want to tell you now is that I feel I have a foothold on its farthest edge. . . . The system of thought, or at least chunks of it, is now emplanted in my mind. I was going to say "in my unconscious mind," and that is what I mean, but I can also ex-amine the pattern consciously. In a sense that is perhaps just a figure of speech, Edenshaw's system of thought, as expressed in his art and myth, is now emplanted [sic] in my mind. And I think at the moment at least, in mine only.[6]

I know that some of Wilson's colleagues thought he placed too much importance in the person and life, and perhaps even the art, of Charles Edenshaw and his uncle, Edward Edenshaw of Massett ("the one great mind that was the two Edenshaws"), but if there was a mystery in Duff's obsession with the Edenshaws, the clue to it is in this letter, which con-tinues:

Lilo, in your philosophy of Heaven and Earth, is there any place for such a kind of reincarnation? Edenshaw would have thought it possible.[7] In fact, I think that one of the meanings of his greatest paintings (the box) is that he could have willed it. Did I ever tell you before that in 1954, when I was on the Charlottes salvaging totem poles, an old lady of his family gave me a name, and I later found out that it was the name he had before he became Edenshaw?

. . . I continue to revel in the subtlety and humour of that marvellous old man Charlie Edenshaw. He is my main teacher, because he purposely made explicit in his work many of the relationships that were only implicit in the earlier art. He wanted us (me?) to see it, but wasn't able to put it into words.

In her letter of 16 March 1974, Lilo Berliner replied:

Yes, I believe in reincarnation and in miracles and in an often imperceivable design which runs from the microcosm to the macrocosm and includes all our "rambles." In German, to ramble is often called "*spinnen*," which refers to the spider web, and what could have more design than that?. . . I also believe in the system of the *I Ching*.

On 30 March, Wilson sent his first poem; it was, he said, "a little Haida rejoinder to Heraclitus," and he called it "You will not go down twice to the same river." On 12 April another poem arrived:

Dear Lilo: We have a fine sense of timing, you and I. All yesterday I spent in writing a poem (my second) whose title from the first draft on would be nothing but "Death Is a Lie." Today's mail brings me your pictures of the exceedingly beautiful little flower which grows best in graveyards. I dedicate my poem to your little flower, although it was originally inspired by something I saw in a Haida design.

What he saw in the design must have been a message from Edenshaw. The poem begins:

If I know
(as I do know)
that I have received, in this life,
a message
sent long ago, during another life;
a secret message,
sent only once,
known only to the sender:
then I know
that the message I have received
must be from myself.

Lilo, 12 April:

I received the first message too and have been infatuated with
it and also much feared it, but never had the courage or the
sense to see it your way. . . .

A silence ensued until 17 July when Wilson wrote to explain that
he had been moving back to his old house, preparing the way for his
sabbatical, and that "we have had Professor Lévi-Strauss with us for the
past two weeks and there have been a number of seminars, the final one
yesterday. He is a marvellous man, and I treasure him as a model of
intellectual audacity."

He then went on to describe his extremely ambitious writing plans.
Perhaps, like most writers, he had to have a long agenda to convince
himself that, though suffering may be long, life is short, and the *oeuvre*
must first be imagined before it can be realized.

There is an article on Haida for the new *Handbook of North
American Indians*. There is a Haida handbook for the Provincial
Museum. A book on Charlie Edenshaw's late masterpieces,
mostly in argillite, is taking shape. So is one which I will call
Mostly About Indians, based on my course this past year and
including student writings, my "teaching story," "Nothing Comes
Only In Pieces," and visuals by Edenshaw. The main work on

the theory of Haida art will proceed, but it is such a large subject that I cannot quite see its shape yet, whether a book or several articles. The catalog for the stone sculpture show is coming along. The list makes me terribly frightened.

As well it might. This, by the way, is the first reference to the stone images show in the existing letters. Also mentioned for the first time is the name of Collyne, one of his students from a Tlingit-speaking family, who was giving him delight not only because she was the best student he ever had but because she had blossomed into a poet. Lilo, of course, was delighted and excited at the vastness of his plans.

> ...and the theory of Haida art which must be as hard and para-
> doxical to write about as Zen because I think that is really the
> core. (I really had not meant to write that because it is none of
> my business to decide and I have a tendency to put everything
> into the framework I decide to set up for it, whether right or
> wrong.) Now that I have trespassed I might as well add that the
> Edenshaw designs have become indispensable to me and I think
> that on certain very fortunate occasions I could see into them
> and get a kind of *satori* with all the answers to all the questions.

I wonder if Wilson picked up what I, in my innocence, think is a profound insight. Certainly Wilson worked a good deal from intuition and instinct, as his poems—and the audacity of his thought—prove. Though he may not have reduced Haida art to a Zen koan, he might have wished to gather it all into a gnomic verbal equation, such as, "I am you. That is you," or into "a tiny, innocuous $E=mc^2$."

His poems, too, were getting shorter, and on 6 November he sent off some more, unsigned, with no return address, and some of Collyne's poems. Lilo wrote (20 November), "Collyne's poems are miracles to me. I still cannot believe that they are here next to me, nor that they were here when I returned from work today, nor that they will be here for ever. . . ." And "I was surprised and delighted with your 'double stand-ards' and 'act of love.' But you always surprise me."

A Wilson letter of 18 November crossed with one of Lilo's (they both seemed to enjoy the idea of letters "crossing"), which contained snippets of Collyne's poetry and the information that "apart from the anguish of writing, my life for the past couple of months has been a surfeit of delights. . . ." And he continues:

> I can see how to think now: in unfettered analogies. I have found my mood and think it is my country's mood: reticent passion. I think I recognize the basic problem: death. I have found the analogy which will allow me to accept it: sharing. I know what I have to do about it: pay back the debt. I can choose my ways of paying it all back.

An increasing note of anguish was registered in Wilson's letter of 30 November:

> Your letters comfort me and puzzle me and do me a great amount of good and don't do me much good, and the truth is that it doesn't matter a hell of lot what is on the page, it's what is in the "eye" of the reader that creates the meaning. . . . Borges said, "Time is the substance I am made of," but he was only half right; there is another ingredient dancing as Time's partner. I think it is Wish. . . . I fear there is really only one wish, and all the others are just echoes of it. To deny death. Its million masks are our celebrations of life.

And then he quotes a new-born poem in two drafts, "Lay down together / two pieces of wood" and continues on about "the real, raw Wish." On a separate page he writes:

> I guess, Lilo, it will be different soon. We'll meet in Victoria. You will see me. I will see you. Your eye will see with its lifetime of conditioning. My eye will see as it is its habit to see.

4 December:

> Dear Wilson: Thank you for your letter. I shall never be able to answer it properly, so am sending you nothing immediately.

(Wish it were Nothing.) Please come when you feel like it. Lilo. I am glad about your 130 stone images!

On 13 January 1975 he mailed a sheaf of poems dated in ink, "January 8/ 75" to "Lilo, my 'twin.' " The title poem, "There is No Such Thing As Going Too Far," disappeared into the xeroxed face of a stone mask with closed eyes which served as a cover. This was one of the great twin masks to be reunited for the exhibition, "Images Stone b.c." Its double, to be brought back from Paris to Victoria by Wilson, had open eyes. A note was enclosed with the poems:

> Dear Lilo: A few more sparks from the wheel. The catalogue for "Images Stone b.c." is finished except for the mask from Paris which I am leaving on Friday to get.
> I am exhausted from it, and can't tell how good it is right now. You will recognize that a little part in it is dedicated to you. Now I am working on the interpretive panels for the exhibit.
> [in handwriting] The trouble with being high on inspiration is that it all seems so flat when you come down.
> Love, Wilson

And Lilo, 18 January:

> Your sparks are like neatly labeled boxes where I can sort out and arrange all my lives.

On 15 February, Wilson sent her a signed invitation to the opening of the exhibition on Tuesday, 4 March, and a letter:

> I have been completely submerged in this business, but now everything has fallen into place. When I brought the second mask home from Paris, the result was even more perfect than we had imagined, as the enclosed xerox images show.[8] There is a special section in it called "Postscript,"[9] which you will recognize as being especially for you. . . .

Why am I still sad? . . . Is there no such thing as having enough?

19 February, Lilo:

> I do not know how you put so much into one envelope and one page. Your twin masks are overwhelming. It took me a while to grasp them and now they have me completely. And somehow I was not prepared for their ears. . . . Watching it all happen is a miracle I cannot quite face except through absurdities, but I am totally aware of the miracles and deeply grateful. All my love, Lilo

Lilo did not use the invitation. And they did not meet. But she must have visited the show almost immediately after the opening, for by Saturday she had paid her second visit:

> This morning I went on your postscript looking and feeling the pieces exactly as you suggested. It was magnificent beyond anything I can express. Perhaps that is the most important meaning of the twins for me. . . . I have no words to thank you, although I know I will need to write you constantly about the images until I die. It must be good to die thinking of the twins. . . . I do not understand how you could have written anything so beautiful, and yet I recognize the chronology of your poems and your letters. I wish I could wrap up the whole world and send it to you, which would be a magnificently absurd act because I know it is all yours anyhow. It would also be rude, because I think you have just given it to me.
>
> I think I know why you talked of sadness in your last letter. I too feel very sad and wish I could weep. Perhaps later. It is right that it is raining and the beach sad and beautiful. First thing this morning the sea otter was on my favourite rock. Then flocks and flocks of turnstones wheeling and I had never thought of their name before, for they are like your images. . . . All my love, Lilo.

In May she visited the exhibition in Vancouver, which produced a new equation for Wilson by way of a process too complicated to go into here, "Which makes the slave killer the freedom bringer or death bringer or birth bringer." She goes on (29 May 1975): "I have fallen in love with that club [see Duff, No. 105, "Death Bringer"] but from the front. I cannot stand in front of it without smiling. Like so many other of the figures it has that superb archaic smile. I have been too possessive about the masks and will remember them the way they were in Victoria, when they were mine entirely and I theirs." This was, it appears, the last letter Wilson answered. Lilo continued writing until 24 December 1975. I don't know why the dialogue became a monologue—and then ceased.

Wilson, 3 June 1975:

> Thank you for the slave-killer, freedom-giver equation, which I had not thought of before. I suppose too that the very existence of slaves proves the existence of a concept of freedom, just as the existence of masks proves that there is a concept of identity. After the opening of "Images" in Vancouver I went into a profound slump, from which I have emerged, only to plunge into the same questions to a more profound depth. . . . I am concentrating more and more on the one great mind that was the two Edenshaws, and receive great waves of insight at the same time as I realize that I cannot possibly hope to reach the heights and breadths of their thought.

He also included a "reading list."

> Among my recent reading have been *The Roots of Coincidence* by Koestler, *Thalassa: A Theory of Genitality* by Ferenczi, and *Phallos* by Vanggaard. I have just discovered Gurdjieff, and am now reading Ouspensky's *In Search of the Miraculous* with a great deal of fascination and *déjà vu.*
>
> . . . "My little abstract" [see Duff, No. 6, "Pure Form"] gives me so much comfort; the comfort of the kind and gentle face of Albert Einstein as he quietly tames the terrors of the universe into a tiny, innocuous $E=mc^2$. One of the additional things it is, in addition to being a mask for the navel, is the "nul set" of

mathematics, the box which is nothing in itself but out of which mathematicians generate all numbers both real and imaginary.

It is also, as you have guessed, the box containing the four other boxes, which is inside the fifth box. All is well, as slavery proves that we can be free.

I have the feeling that I am almost ready to state Duff's Law. It will be an equation, with "I am You. That is You" on the one hand, and "The World is As Sharp As A Knife" on the other. The world is a single twin, caught in the reciprocal act: Love, Wilson.

Wilson kept xeroxed copies of this letter. In September Lilo left for her rock art camping trip. Her last letter began: "I have saved this letter for Christmas Eve because writing to you is my best Christmas present to myself. As usual, I can offer you nothing except my very invisible wishes."

Before she died, Lilo and I had discussed the possibility of doing something with Wilson's letters. The night she walked into the sea she left them in a black plastic bag on my doorstep. They were her bequest to me. Wilson Duff's daughter, Marnie, gave me Lilo Berliner's letters so that I could fulfill what I felt must be Lilo's intention.

In this correspondence both Lilo and Wilson went beyond the masks of dailiness. Although twins, they were not identical. Wilson agreed with Ouspenski that "art is mathematics"; Lilo saw art as life and life as a series of epiphanies. Where Wilson's mind searched diadic structures for "the two hands of God," Lilo listened for the sound of one hand clapping and heard it in spirals and circles. For Lilo the doctrine of correspondences—as above, so below—informed her universe. She was a Jungian and oriental. Wilson was a Freudian and western. Even the ways in which they chose to end their lives continued each one's catalogues of awesome symbols. And perhaps it was the discovery of two stone masks nesting in great art that ultimately kept them from meeting.

All I really know is that some of their best friends were dead. I met Wilson only twice, but I had known Lilo for years. When she walked into the sea on that January night of the full moon to join her friends, she was, I am sure, wearing, if nothing else, "a hint of Frog's wry smile."[10]

1977

[1] Wilson Duff, "Personal Communication, June 12, 1972, not for quotation but for information and feedback."

[2] See his *Images Stone b.c.* "The great French anthropologist Claude Lévi-Strauss has shown that the 'savage mind' is really a scientific mind that uses natural images rather than abstract symbols to create what he calls a 'science of the concrete.' I would say that the artist-thinkers of the North-West Coast had created a sort of 'mathematics of the concrete,' which by the time the white man arrived had become an 'advanced mathematics.'"

[3] In the letters titles of books, articles, and poems have been standardized. Spelling and punctuation have not been changed. Square brackets indicate my comments.

[4] This concern with Nothing is not so extraordinary. Cf. a Genesis story from Jerome Rothenberg's *Technicians of the Sacred* : "A phantasm, nothing else existed in the beginning: the Father touched an illusion, he grasped something mysterious. Nothing existed. Through the agency of a dream our Father Nai-mu-ena kept the mirage to his body, and he pondered long and thought deeply. Nothing existed, not even a stick to support the vision: our Father attached the illusion to the thread of a dream and kept it by the aid of his breath. He sounded to reach the bottom of the appearance, but there was nothing. Nobody existed. Then the Father again investigated the bottom of the mystery. He tied the empty illusion to the dream thread and pressed the magical substance upon it. Then by the aid of his dream he held it like a wisp of raw cotton. Then he seized the mirage bottom and stamped upon it repeatedly, sitting down at last on his dreamed earth. The Earth-phantasm was his now, and he spat out saliva repeatedly so that the forests might grow. Then he lay down on his earth and covered it with the roof of heaven. As he was the owner of the earth he placed above it the blue and the white sky. Thereupon Rafu-ema, the-man-who-has-the-narratives, sitting at the base of the sky, pondered, and he created his story so that he might listen to it here upon earth." (Columbia, Uitoto Indians)

[5] The way John Sky told it, according to Chini Sol, Raven dug a hole for the eyes in the fire, mixed them with ashes, and ate them. "And when he ate them, they gave out a little sound, like a popping sound. And he laughed when he ate them."

[6] See Lévi-Strauss, *The Raw and the Cooked*: "[I]t is in the last resort immaterial whether in this book the thought processes of the South American Indians take shape through the medium of my thought, or whether mine takes place through the medium of theirs."

[7] See Duff: "We do not know the name of the maker of the masks, nor any of that artist's earlier names. But I think I know his last one: Edenshaw" (22).

[8] The masks "nested" together. See Duff: "The culminating image of thirty centuries of stone sculpture is really about the glint of recognition, which is the purest pulse of life. Eyes of the past and eyes of the future meet and there is a thrill of recognition the instant they both see that they share an equal hint of Frog's wry smile." Frog, according to Duff, was a crest, "but something more as well, it had become one of the main actors in a system of logical paradoxes, the exploration of which was one of the most active hidden agendas of the art. Frog became— or so it seems to me—a convenient and friendly opposite-sign; part sublime but part absurd. . . ." (148).

[9] Actually "Epilogue," see Duff (165-66).

[10] See Duff, 148-9, also 165.

Tibetan Deϑire

That night, did I wear red nail polish? If I did, it wasn't called "Tibetan Desire." That was the name of the nail polish F chose in *Beautiful Losers*—"such a contradiction in terms"—to paint a plastic model of the Acropolis red, with the tiny brush.

It "gleamed like a huge ruby" as the narrator and F lay looking at it in the glow of the soft morning beyond, and when they squinted "it burst into a cool lovely fire, sending out rays in all directions. . . Don't weep, F said, and we began to talk."

It was the sixties. I was in Montreal for some reason I now forget, not the Chelsea Hotel, not the Acropolis either. Leonard Cohen had come to guide me through my first unnatural high. Was I wearing red nail polish? Was I going to see the world as a huge ruby bursting into fire?

We lit up. You've got to see Ste. Catherine Street, L said. And then we'll go and have Chinese food. It tastes fantastic.

Nothing's happening.

It will.

I puffed. He waited patiently. Not the Chelsea Hotel. Not a huge ruby. A grid moving on my right shoulder blade, a *grid*, eyes at the back of my head. You're there, you're high, or some such words. Giggling, conspiratorial, we set out for the cool night beyond. We wandered along the sainted street reacting to movie posters, shop windows, people, neon signs, happy, hungry, elevated, heading for the ultimate taste sensation of Montreal Chinese food.

I'd first met L back in the fifties at Irving Layton's house in Côte St. Luc. Louis Dudek had brought his protegé at the time they were preparing *Let Us Compare Mythologies* for Contact Press. I remember being surprised to learn that Leonard, who seemed so young, was voluntarily studying the Bible as an informal ongoing project. How that old Christian fascination has kept pace with his consciousness de-formations still puzzles me, is still insistently summoned, rock of ages, in his latest album, *The Future*.

Who was there? Or who was usually there, because I don't remember the exact line-up the night of L's arrival. Betty Layton, of course, radiant and smiling, always a luminous presence, and a wonderful friend to me; the Layton children, Maxie and Naomi (Sissyboo), and Irving, who tried to sell us his latest books, who read his spectacular poems. Miriam Waddington occasionally appeared, and Frank Scott, Al Purdy, Gael Turnbull, Eli Mandel, Avi Boxer, Aileen Collins, Louise Scott, Robert Currie, others. The Layton living-room was small, but it never felt crowded; the talk was lively and spontaneous, poems got batted about, L's being the most freshly lyrical and genuinely sensuous, I think I thought. Leonard was trying Law School at McGill, though he'd soon drop out. It must have felt strange to him to have Frank Scott, professor of constitutional law, greet him in such an informal setting. But our youngest poet was even then suave and cool and collected, on the outside, at least. There's always been a space around him. Sometimes it lets you in, sometimes it doesn't.

I was soon to leave for a year in London, but when I came back I saw Leonard from time to time. One night we'd gone out for a drive and ended up at his mother's house where he was staying. That's when he introduced me to mangoes and talked about the young woman he was in love with. I wrote a poem about the mango experience, revising it some years later:

Revision

I slice the flesh of an old poem
I started for you in 1957
called "Mangoes for Leonard Cohen"
the lines fall away
flesh that is often lost

Now I slice into the luminous
mangoes like a surgeon
the delight in my eyes

as they behold the broken tissue
is the delight of the skillful surgeon. . . .

My other recollections are of the more professional times we spent together in Toronto when I worked for the CBC. Memories of having coffee at the Four Seasons Hotel across the street from the studio when L showed me the notebook he always carried with him, the poems and songs, the multiple revisions. Listening to him and watching as he recorded poems for the 1966 CBC two-LP album *Canadian Poets I*. Another time there was a private concert at the Park Plaza Hotel when he sang "Dress Rehearsal Rag," saying he'd never record it. He did, in *Songs of Love and Hate* in 1971.

In 1967, Centennial year, I was doing a series of television programs on contemporary Canadian poetry for the CBC and brought Leonard and Gwen MacEwen together for a half-hour program. I thought it was a dazzling combination. Both of them beautiful and "exotic," both spice-box of earth poets, both mysterious and seductive, regional only in their universalities. The programs were shown at some miserably early hour on Sunday mornings.

I think this professional connection must have begun in Montreal when I interviewed Leonard for CBC radio just after he had returned from Europe where he'd written *Beautiful Losers*. He was still recovering from that experience and I saw a dramatic change in him—a wilder, more battered L, sunstroked from writing outside in the Grecian light.

The radio and TV meetings ended when I left the CBC in 1969 and returned to the west coast. So did our friendship. I never heard from him again.

But recently (summer 1993) he re-entered my consciousness very powerfully. He was scheduled to give a concert in Victoria, B.C. on 19 June at the Royal Theatre. I'd never actually seen him in concert and I decided I must go. Stephen Scobie was able to nab a ticket for me and a pass for backstage after the show. It was a great evening, a great concert promoting *The Future*, the visual effects reminding me of German Expressionist painting (I've seen the past and it is murder). He didn't seem to recognize me when we met, which seemed so strange as to be laughable. It had *only* been twenty-five years or so since we'd seen each other, after all. He got the scene right, though: Montreal, Irving's house, Betty Layton, a key reference, so many dead. Perhaps he just couldn't recall my name after a European tour and a three-hour songfest. Or just refused to say Phyllis. (I never ever wanted to call him Len or Lennie.)

But that was not the end of it. There was Helga. I'd been billeted at her home when I was attending a conference in Essen a few years ago. Helga is what you call a fan, of Cohen's, of Canada. In the Canada Suite in her house she has a signed photo of him, along with autographed photos of Omar Sharif, Brian Mulroney and Mila, Pierre Trudeau, Joe Clarke and Maureen, etc. L is, I suspect, Helga's soul-mate, his songs an accompaniment to her life as wife, mother, former fashion model, executive member of the German Canadian Society in Dusseldorf. Suddenly, Helga decides to visit me at the end of July after delivering some exchange students to Toronto. And Leonard Cohen will be doing a return engagement in Victoria on 30 July, I tell her. It's her thirtieth wedding anniversary, but her husband is understanding, and her daughter encourages her to take this opportunity because she missed *The Future* concert when L was in Germany. Stephen Scobie is rounded up to work his magic at getting tickets (he'd also stayed in the Canada Suite on one of his jaunts). He's able to seat her in the front row and take her backstage to meet L. She will present him with—as she'd done in 1988 at his *I'm Your Man* concert in Montreal—a single red rose, glowing like a huge ruby.

That night when I was either wearing red nail polish or not wearing red nail polish, on the way back to the hotel I fell into a depression L was concerned about because, he said as we parted, a marijuana low is really serious. But I was used to depression, no doubt more comfortable with natural lows than unnatural highs. He didn't say, "Don't weep." He hadn't written that book yet. I was touched by his attentiveness to my mood change and grateful for his sense of responsibility as guide on my round about trip.

After the 29 June concert, backstage, I thought Leonard exhibited an extraordinary Buddhistic calm, the space around him larger, more defined now by professional distance. Stephen thought he was just plain tired. You still don't remember me, I teased. Of course I do, darlin'. I wasn't quite convinced, something hadn't clicked. Then the space collapsed briefly as he gave me a warm hug, his post-performance bodyheat a cool lovely fire passing through me on its way to Tibet.

1994

Message Machine

"Psychopomp," what a nice, round, fat word. It arrived like a bird on the wing, a plump robin; it brushed my ear, dropped down to the lawn for a worm, zoomed past again, "Psychopomp," blurred by and out of sight. Roger, over and out, and I wrote it down, mysterious word, full of circumstance. But what did it mean? I thought of that time I'd heard it, years ago, uttered by Norman O. Brown on a tape he'd recorded for a CBC program we were preparing on the theme of reconciliation. I knew vaguely that Psychopomp was connected with Mercury, god of messenger services and thieves, fleet-footed Mercury with wings on his heels. I checked my reference books. Psychopomp was Mercury in his guise as escort of dead souls to the Underworld. He also brought Persephone back to her mother, Ceres. That's it, I said, and was on my way to a poem.

But what has this to do with feminism? I try to allow these words that arrive unbidden to lead me into poems, and have been using this sort of intense listening as a conscious process for about two years now. I've had to ask myself a few questions about this procedure. Although there may well be a neurological explanation for the way autonomous words, phrases, and sentences arrive apparently at random, unconnected to my preoccupations of the moment, I doubt that any research has been done on this sort of fine-tuning of the inner ear. Most frequently I ask myself: is this process too passive to be politically correct? Does it reflect more accurately than I'd care to admit the laid-back, unwilled, apolitical position of the supine female of all those nudes and odalisques of so many paintings from the cultural "patrimony," as PEN describes our cultural inheritance? I would not have thought of asking such a question twenty or so years ago, would have preferred some romantic explanation about inspiration. But for me, a minimalist producer, there's also a practical side to such self-criticism: would I produce more poems if I were not always hanging around for the right moment, listening for "the bird song in the apparatus," to quote myself?

Another question I'm immediately aware of as I let Psychopomp lead the way is, oh dear, why has old psyche thrown up yet another male figure, attractive, ambiguous, quick-silvery though he may be? In typing that sentence, instead of oh dear I typed oh dead—Psychopomp at work in the black humour market. I do *not* want mythological figures in my poems, especially as subjects, foregrounding, subjecting personages. I'm trying to cultivate a curvilinear, or else an oblique, angled, perverse method, even polymorphous, like prose poems, to refer again to N. O. Brown (*Love's Body* 1966).

I'm off. I go with the rush, get something down as fast as I can. I'll think about these serious matters later. Fully engaged in this pleasurable activity, I don't even notice that I'm writing a feeble little poem, echoing a past style, more elegant and accomplished, perhaps, than any draft thirty years ago. Perhaps not.

"Psychopomp"

The escort has wings
on his feet
he walks fast
for fear of flying

he drags me along
for a song
towards the unkempt
graves of Hades

there's an ace
up his sleeve
he snitched it
from the dead-pan
poker player

clouds drift away
at the sound
of his poppy breath

are we up or down
head over heels
like clowns

are we travelling light
mercurial
towards transfiguration?

Oh dear, which I type correctly this time. There she is, poor girl, being dragged by this speedy macho type off to the Underworld. Do I even believe in the Underworld? No matter, an archetypal image, the psychic equivalent of the China Syndrome, and like Alice in Wonderland, kerplunk, I'm there, was there while writing the tinkly lines. Why are you so hard on yourself? a small voice sighs, and the counter-tenor responds, look at that narrator of yours, and a first-person narrator too, like some rape victim being towed along on a journey she's only too willing to take. Typical masochistic Harlequin stuff. Chuck it! Complete with exclamation mark.

The voices are becoming confusing. Here's one that says Wait. Let's look at this whole thing more carefully. Is there a message here as in a dream, perhaps a reversal, disguise, androgynous bi-play?

An interpretation, I'm not against it. I am not "me." I'm really Psychopomp. Cross-dressing would be one way of describing this transformation now. Then who is telling the tale? As in dream interpretation, she could *also* be me, but I go for clues from the more immediate attentions of my life. I have a very old mother in her nineties who jokes she's still thirty-nine. Trying to be the good daughter, that too, wanting to ease somewhat the pain and boredom of her days, I frequently take her out for lunch or a drive, which I've no doubt done not so long before writing this poem. I wish I could say that my car is a Ford Mercury. I feel the wings sprouting at my heels, tickling. Hi, I'm Psychopomp from the Escort Service. No wonder in the poem I write of transfiguration; what else is the deep wish, the inspiration of cross-dressing, masquerade, street theatre?

Not such an anti-feminist poem as it seemed at first glance. Unfortunately, the dream-type analysis does not improve the poem—notice, for instance, that missing beat in the fourth stanza.

These conscious questionings of my own passivity have, I realize now, been more pervasive over the last two years than I'd noticed. Take the most extraordinary, for me, of my given phrases, "the salt tax." Where did it come from, why? I heard it very clearly for the first time on 8 September 1988. It was followed by "paradigm shift" and "cosmic rays" on 12 September, "seeing is believing" on the thirteenth and fourteenth, and "the cedar trees" on the fifteenth. I knew what the salt tax was and had been greatly moved when I was young by Gandhi's person and his philosophy of passive resistance, Satyagraha, but the phrase seemed unpromising as an entry into a poem. Even with all those other phrases beaming in, an unusual number of them, "the salt tax" recurred insistently, and I finally wrote the poem on 17 September. (See *Hanging Fire*, 1990). Appropriately, it's a sort of sound poem, with musical reference to Philip Glass, the composer of the opera *Satyagraha*. It is, I hope, not too far-fetched to suggest that the poem commemorating Gandhi's trek to the sea to protest the salt tax, "to steal a handful of free-ee-ee-dom," is in some subliminal way dealing with my own passivity, offering reconciliation. The hooking together of "passive" and "resistance" with such a neat paradoxical click made a supremely useful political slogan that's had a long life. It tells me again that some kinds of passive behaviour are productive of real change, social and otherwise.

One of my discoveries during the past two years is that the given words I've chosen to work from are thematically connected, that the strategies of the unconscious are very subtle and certainly not random if you watch the test patterns long enough. Countering the passive mood of some of the poems are those dealing with the Marxian class struggle, animal rights, violent revolution, if only by means of glancing blows. This dialectic goes deep in my nature, explaining or rationalizing my characteristic ambivalence about all things great and small.

The post-facto analytical intelligence sometimes performs with cool accomplished reserve, sometimes, like Glenn Gould, humming along with the music. There are other times when a gleeful and spiteful intentionality slashes a line across the page, knocks the cliché on the head, kicks the dogma under the table. Oh dead. I've resisted writing this essay for months, possibly because my instinct to subvert the assigned exercise collided with my good daughter mode. I didn't want to ring the party line. After I decided I might as well give up on the attempt, and as the dead-line approached ever closer, I turned on the message machine: Hi, I'm Psychopomp, pomp, pomp, pomp—et voilà, I made it. My last two given phrases, by the way, were "Self City" and "Anaximander"—not again!

1990

And Things Get Stranger
Every Day

Vancouver Island is weighing anchor, heading for the South Pacific. At the corner of Government and Belleville streets in Victoria the carillon chimes out, "Goodbye Canada, Goodbye." The great island makes a stately flagship, a flotilla of smaller Gulf Islands following in its wake. Passengers and crew are in a holiday mood. Politicians lounge in deck chairs sipping fruit juice. Civil servants head "up island" for Long Beach as members of the Nootka tribe race south to liberate artifacts in the Royal Provincial Museum. Tourists in Butchart Gardens sniff the sea air and strike up shipboard romances. On Little Saanich Mountain, concerned with higher things, astronomers at the Astrophysical Observatory shift their sights for new supernova. But Oak Bay golfers are dismayed, for among sportsmen, as Irving Layton has said, "they are the metaphysicians / intent, untalkative, pursuing Unity."

It's a charming fantasy for a west coast rainy day. I had it often during the Meech Lake debate, and here we go again, flags flying. But this is no ordinary South Pacific cruise. As we glide by Fiji, hot and prickly in our winter clothes, the rain forest in even deeper shock than usual, some of us begin to long for home.

Fax rumours abound. The P.M. placed a call. He's finally noticed. He hasn't. He has. The *Globe and Mail* is going tabloid. Denied. Affirmed. Quebec wants to know if we're speaking French yet. Anything but—Cantonese, Japanese, Vietnamese, American. The Four Seasons Hotel in Vancouver is being torn down to make way for a new legislature to replace Victoria's. No! We're losing power, losing touch with Kamloops, Lytton, Hope, Fort St. John, *Toronto.* We experience a rush of solidarity with Newfoundland out there on the fringe. Suddenly we miss the constitutional committees, cabinet shuffles, the CBC.

And things get stranger every day. The sea around us throbs with dying dolphins who cry out their problems as if we were friends. The flotilla is spreading out and spreading thin. On Salt Spring Island the

Buddhist retreat recruits dozens of loggers every day. In the woods deer are miniaturizing in Darwinian fast forward; tiny cougars pad around shrub-like Douglas firs. Multinational corporations devolve into cowrie shells, and politicians know for sure small isn't beautiful. For God's sake, Captain, head back home before we all incredibly shrink!

Lights on the Parliament Buildings surge on. "Power, Power, Power," they flash to guide us past Hawaii and on and up into the blue dark coastal night.

We arrive just in time for Canada's one hundred twenty-fifth, re-freshed by our new perspectives, younger and wiser. Ships of the B.C. Ferries fleet, circling in fog and confusion all this time, aim for our docks where they're greeted with wild cheers. What's the point of being an islander if you can't get off to the mainland now and then? But the golf-ers stay put, resume their game, like good Canadians, pursuing Unity.

1992

Works Cited

Ackroyd, Peter. *T.S. Eliot*. London: Hamish Hamilton, 1984.

Alexander, Paul. *Rough Magic, A Biography of Sylvia Plath*. Harmondsworth: Penguin Books, 1992.

Allen, Donald and Warren Tallman. *Poetics of the New American Poetry*. New York: Grove Press, 1973.

Barbeau, Marius. "Haida Myths Illustrated in Argillite Carvings," *Bulletin No. 127*, Anthropological Series No. 32 (1953), National Museum of Canada.

Barbour, Douglas. *Shore Lines*. Winnipeg: Turnstone Press, 1979.

Barthes, Roland. *The Pleasure of the Text*. Translated by Richard Miller, with a Note on the text by Richard Howard. New York: Hill and Wang, 1975.

Blaser, Robin. *The Holy Forest*. Introduction by Robert Creeley. Toronto: Coach House, 1993.

Bond, Alma Halbert. *Who Killed Virginia Woolf? A Psychobiography*. New York: Human Sciences Press, Insight Books, 1989.

Bowering, George. "The Breath, Release." In *15 Canadian Poets Plus 5*, edited by Gary Geddes and Phyllis Bruce. Toronto: Oxford University Press, 1978.

Cohen, Leonard. *The Energy of Slaves*. Toronto: McClelland and Stewart, 1972.

Dante. *The Divine Comedy, 1: Hell*. Translated by Dorothy L. Sayers. Harmondsorth: Penguin Books, 1949.

_____. *The Divine Comedy: Paradiso*. Translated by Laurence Binyon. *The Portable Dante*. Edited by Paolo Milano. New York: The Viking Press, 1947.

De Salvo, Louise. *Virginia Woolf: The Impact of Childhood Sexual Abuse on Her Life and Works*. New York: Ballantine Books, 1989.

Dickinson, Emily. *The Complete Poems*. Edited by Thomas H. Johnson. Boston: Little, Brown and Company, 1960.

Duff, Wilson. *Images Stone b.c.* Saanichton, B. C.: Hancock House, 1975.

Duncan, Robert. Taped interview with Phyllis Webb. Vancouver, 1963.

_____. "Keeping the Rhyme." In *The Opening of the Field*. New York: Grove Press, 1960.

Edel, Leon. *Bloomsbury: A House of Lions*. New York: Avon Books, 1979.

Eliot, T.S. *Selected Poems*. Harmondsworth: Penguin Books, 1948.

Erikson, Erik H. *Young Man Luther: A Study in Psychoanalysis and History*. London: Faber and Faber, 1958.

Freud, Sigmund. *Three Essays on the Theory of Sexuality*. Translated and edited by James Strachey. New York: Avon Books, 1962.

_____. "Leonardo da Vinci and a Memory of His Childhood." In *The Standard Edition of the Complete Psychological Works of Sigmund Freud*, Vol. 11. London: Hogarth Press.

Funk and Wagnalls Standard Dictionary of the English Language. Britannica World Language Edition. New York: Funk and Wagnalls, 1960.

Gay, Peter. *Freud: A Life for Our Times*. New York: W.W. Norton, 1988.

Gide, André. *The Journals of André Gide*, Vol. 1, 1889-1913. Translated with an Introduction and Notes by Justin O'Brien. London: Secker and Warburg, 1947.

Gilbert, Sandra M. and Susan Gubar. *The Madwoman in the Attic*. New Haven: Yale University Press, 1979.

Graves, Robert. *The White Goddess*. New York: Vintage Press, 1960.

Hill, Beth and Ray Hill. *Indian Petroglyphs of the Pacific Northwest*. Saanichton, B. C.: Hancock House, 1974.

Jacobs, Arthur. *A New Dictionary of Music*. Harmondsworth: Penguin Books, 1971.

Jaynes, Julian. *The Origin of Consciousness in the Breakdown of the Bicameral Mind*. Toronto: University of Toronto Press, 1976.

Joyce, James. *Portrait of the Artist as a Young Man*. In *The Essential James Joyce*. Introduction and Notes by Harry Levin. London: Jonathan Cape, 1948. See pages 176-177.

Karl, Frederick, R. *Joseph Conrad: The Three Lives*. New York.: Farrar, Straus and Giroux, 1979.

Kermode, Frank. "The High Cost of New History." Review of *Forms of Nationhood: The Elizabethan Writing of England* by Richard Helgerson. *The New York Review of Books* (June 25, 1992): 43-45.

Koch, Kenneth. "The Boiling Water" and "The Problem of Anxiety." In

The Burning Mystery of Anna in 1951. New York: Random House, 1979.

Kofman, Sarah. *The Childhood of Art: An Interpretation of Freud's Aesthetics*. Translated by Winifred Woodhull. New York: Columbia University Press, 1988.

LaChapelle, Edward R. *Field Guide to Snow Crystals*. Seattle: University of Washington Press, 1969.

Lamb, Charles. *The Works of Charles and Mary Lamb*. In *Elia and The Last Essays of Elia*, Vol. 2, p. 103. Edited by E. V. Lucas. London: Methuen, 1903.

Levertov, Denise. "On the Function of the Line," *Chicago Review*, 30. 3 (Winter 1979): 30-36.

Lévi-Strauss, Claude. *The Raw and the Cooked*, Vol. 1. New York: Harper and Row, Harper Colophon Books, 1975.

Lyly, John. *The Complete Works of John Lyly, Poems, Early Autobiographical*, Vol. 3, p. 452. Edited by R. W. Bond. Oxford at the Clarendon Press, 1902.

McGuire, William, Ed. *The Freud / Jung Letters, The Correspondence Between Sigmund Freud and C. G. Jung*. Translated by Ralph Manheim and R. F. C. Hull. Bollingen Series XCIV. Princeton: Princeton University Press, 1974.

Marcuse, Herbert. *Eros and Civilization, A Philosophical Inquiry into Freud*. New York: Beacon Press, Vintage Books, 1955.

Middlebrook, Diane. *Anne Sexton: A Biography*. Boston: Houghton Mifflin, 1991.

Olson, Charles. Taped interview with Phyllis Webb, Vancouver, 1963.

Ovid. *Metamorphoses*. Translated by Mary M. Innes. Harmondsworth: Penguin Books, 1955.

Peters, H. F. *Rainer Maria Rilke: Masks and the Man*. Seattle: University of Washington Press, 1960.

Pound, Ezra. *ABC of Reading*. New York: W.W. Norton, 1979.

_____. *Literary Essays of Ezra Pound*. Edited by T.S. Eliot. New York: New Directions, 1954.

Proust, Marcel. *Remembrance of Things Past*. Translated by C. K. Moncrieff and Frederick A. Blossom. 2 vols. New York: Random House, 1932.

Rich, Adrienne. *Lies, Secrets and Silence: Selected Prose, 1966-78.* New York: W.W. Norton, 1979.

_____. *The Dream of a Common Language: Poems 1974-77.* New York: W.W. Norton, 1978.

Rilke, Rainer Maria. *The Selected Poetry of Rainer Maria Rilke.* Edited and translated by Stephen Mitchell. New York: Random House, 1982.

Rothenberg, Jerome. *Technicians of the Sacred.* New York: Doubleday, Anchor Books, 1969.

Sanders, Ed. "Investigative Poetry: The Content of History will be Poetry." *Talking Poetics from Naropa Institute*, Vol. 2. Boulder: Shambala, 1979. 365-78.

Sexton, Anne. *The Complete Poems.* Boston: Houghton Mifflin, 1981.

_____. "O Ye Tongues." In *The Death Notebooks.* Boston: Houghton Mifflin, 1974.

Smart, Christopher. *Jubilate Agno.* Edited by W.H. Bond. New York: Greenwood, 1969.

Stevenson, Anne. *Bitter Fame: A Life of Sylvia Plath.* Boston: Houghton Mifflin, 1989.

Strachey, Lytton. *Eminent Victorians.* San Diego: Harcourt Brace, 1969.

Swanton, John R. *Contributions to the Ethnology of the Haida.* New York: American Museum of Natural History, Memoir VIII, Part 1, 1905.

Thesen, Sharon. *Artemis Hates Romance.* Toronto: Coach House, 1980.

_____. *Confabulations: Poems for Malcolm Lowry.* Lantzville, B.C.: Oolichan Books, 1984.

_____. *Holding the Pose.* Toronto: Coach House, 1983.

_____. "A Few Notes on Poetry." *Poetry Canada Review*, 7, 4 (1986).

Thompson, John. *Stilt Jack.* Toronto: House of Anansi, 1978.

Wayman, Tom. *Free Time: Industrial Poems.* Toronto: Macmillan of Canada, 1977.

Webb, Phyllis. "A Bow to the Numinous." *Books in Canada*, (April 1994): 27-8.

_____. *Selected Poems: The Vision Tree.* Edited and with an Introduction by Sharon Thesen. Vancouver: Talonbooks, 1982.

Acknowledgements

The following essays are reprinted from my first prose collection, *Talking* (Quadrant Editions, 1982), now out of print: "Waterlily and Multifoliate Rose: Cyclic Notions in Proust," "On the Line," "Up the Ladder: Notes on the Creative Process," "A Correspondence," and "Phyllis Webb's Canada."

I would like to thank Gary Geddes for permission to reprint his "Letter" from *Talking*.

Other publications include "The Muse Figure," *In the Feminine: Women and Words/Les Femmes et les Mots*; "Unearned Numinosity," *Grain*; "Imaginations Companion," *The Malahat Review*; "Message Machine," *Language in Her Eye: Views on Writing and Gender by Canadian Women Writing in English*; "The Drover's Wife," *Sport* (New Zealand); "And Things Get Stranger Every Day," The Bank of Montreal Annual Report for 1991 and *Maclean's*; "Might-Have-Been: The Tedious Shores," *Brick*; and "Tibetan Desire," *Take This Waltz, A Celebration of Leonard Cohen*.

"Gabrielle Roy's *Windflower*" appeared as the Afterword to *Windflower*, translated by Joyce Marshall (McClelland and Stewart, New Canadian Library, Toronto, 1991), and is reprinted here with the kind permission of McClelland and Stewart and editor David Staines. The essay under its current title was also published in *Brick*.

"Poetry and Psychobiography" was first presented as a lecture for The Vancouver Institute in 1993 and published in *Brick* and *Landfall* (New Zealand).

The reproductions in "The Mind's Eye, A Photo-Collage Essay" are laser prints of the original collages. Laser printing alters the colours somewhat and reduces the glossiness of the actual photographic elements. Another result is that the "joins" are less visible.

Thanks to Coach House Press and Robin Blaser for permission to reprint in full the text of "Image-Nation 1 (the fold" from *The Holy Forest*.

My thanks to Helga Wodrich and Geoff Isherwood for permission to use some photographic elements in the collages.

My gratitude also to those editors who first published these essays, and to Smaro Kamboureli who, as editor of The Writer as Critic Series, greatly assisted and encouraged me in the preparation of the manuscript. Finally, my thanks to Lorna Jackson who produced the disk.

Index

NeWest Press gratefully acknowledges the financial assistance of The Canada Council;
The Alberta Foundation for the Arts, a beneficiary of the Lottery Fund of the Government
of Alberta; and The NeWest Institute for Western Canadian Studies.

COMMITTED TO THE DEVELOPMENT OF CULTURE AND THE ARTS